Love Bites

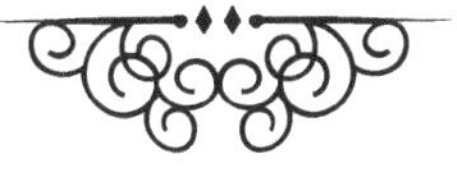

Vol. 2

Joan Booth

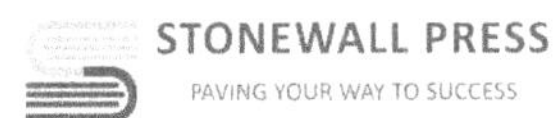

Printed in the United States of America

ISBN 13: Paperback: 978-1-948172-47-9
eBook: 978-1-948172-46-2

Library of Congress Control Number: 2017916698

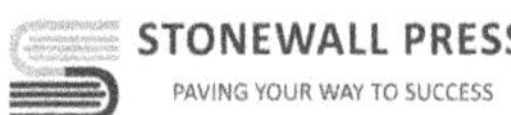

Stonewall Press
363 Paladium Court
Owings Mills, MD 21117
www.stonewallpress.com
1-888-334-0980

For all who have ever loved or been in love.

Contents

Acknowledgements

To A.K., for inspiring this journey of the heart
To Andrew, for his creative contributions

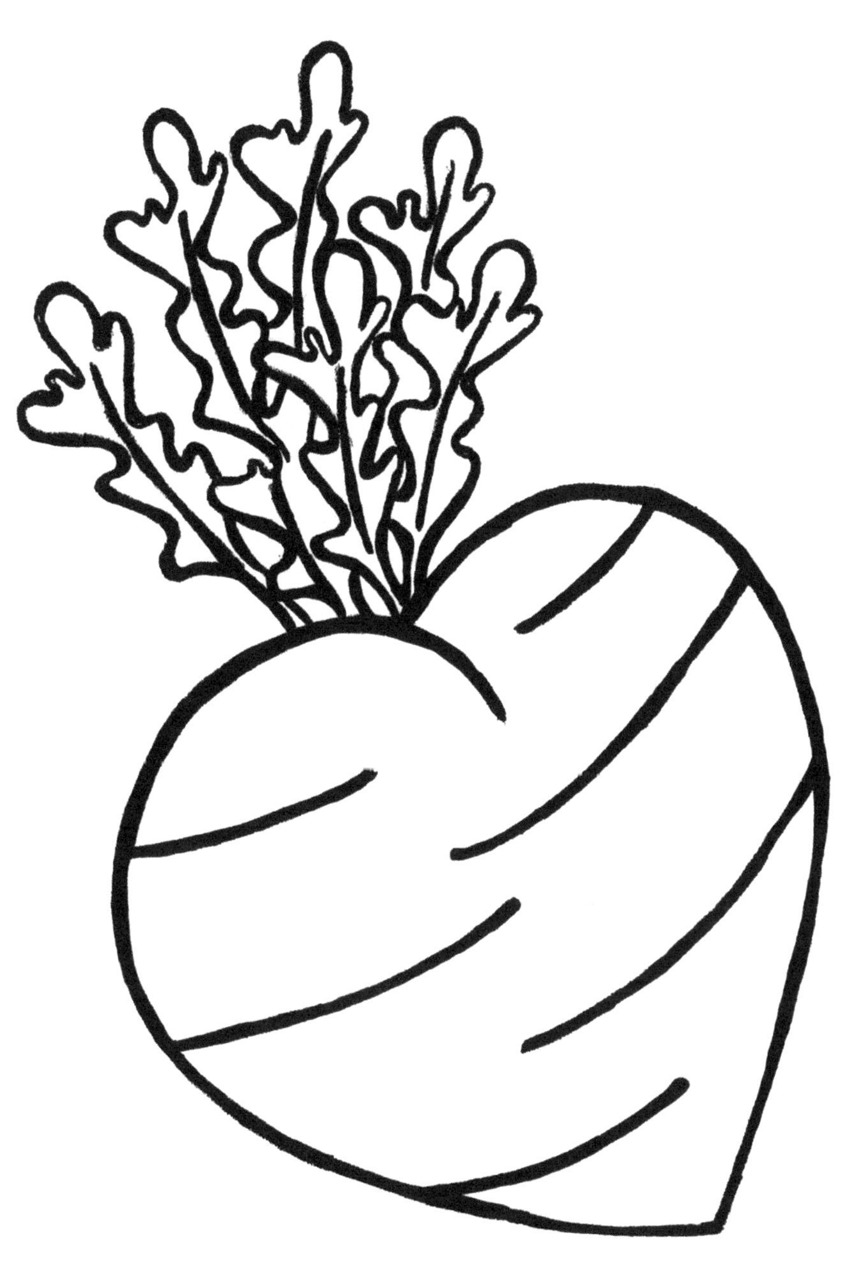

Healthy Love

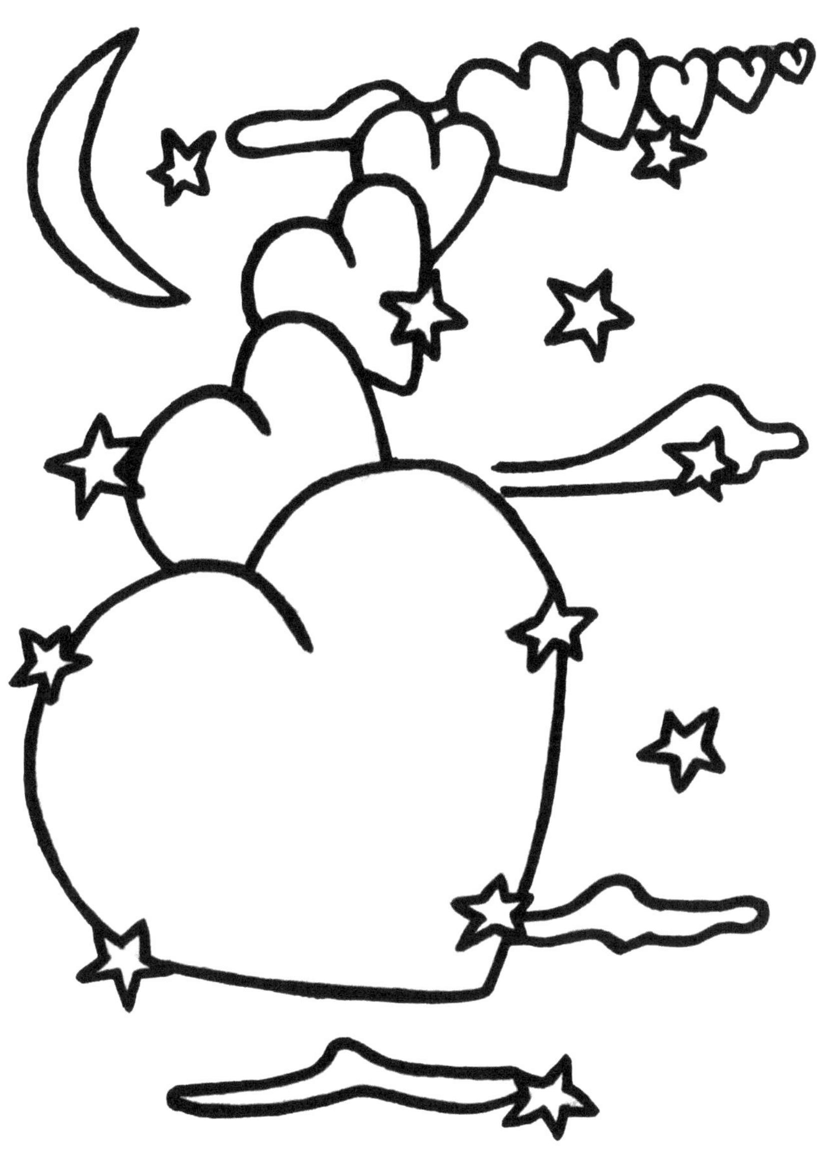

Forever Love

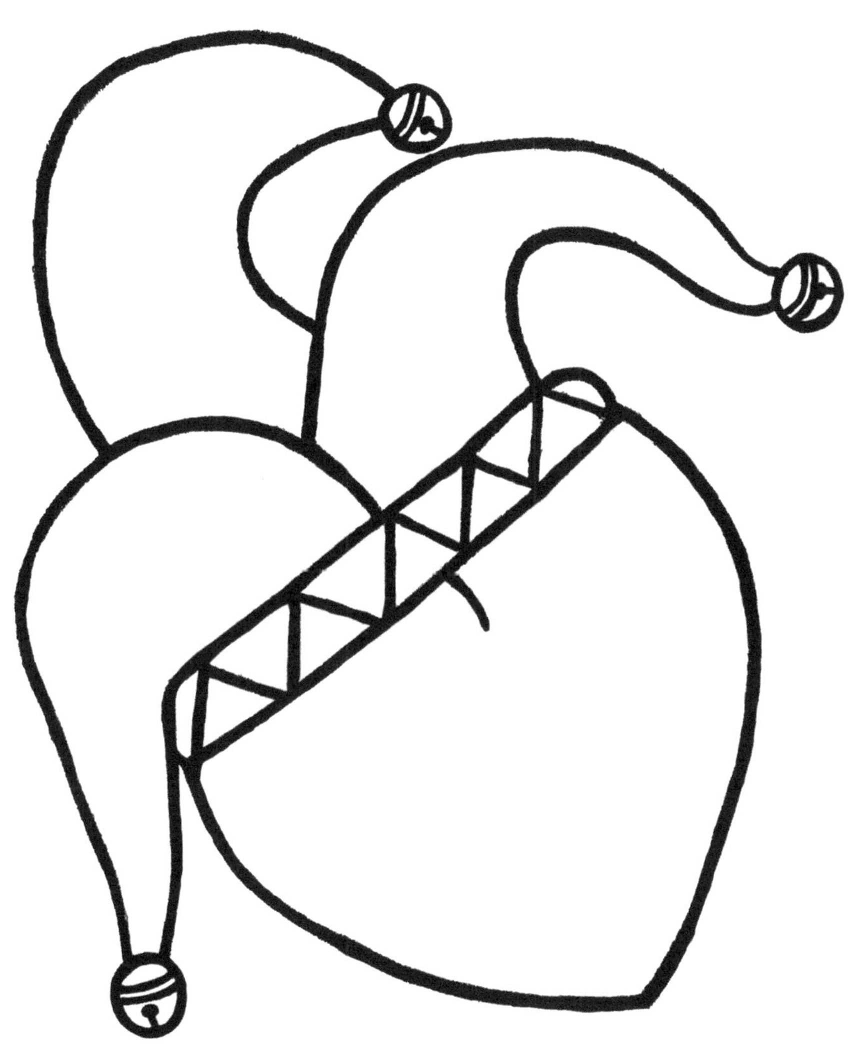

Fool for Love

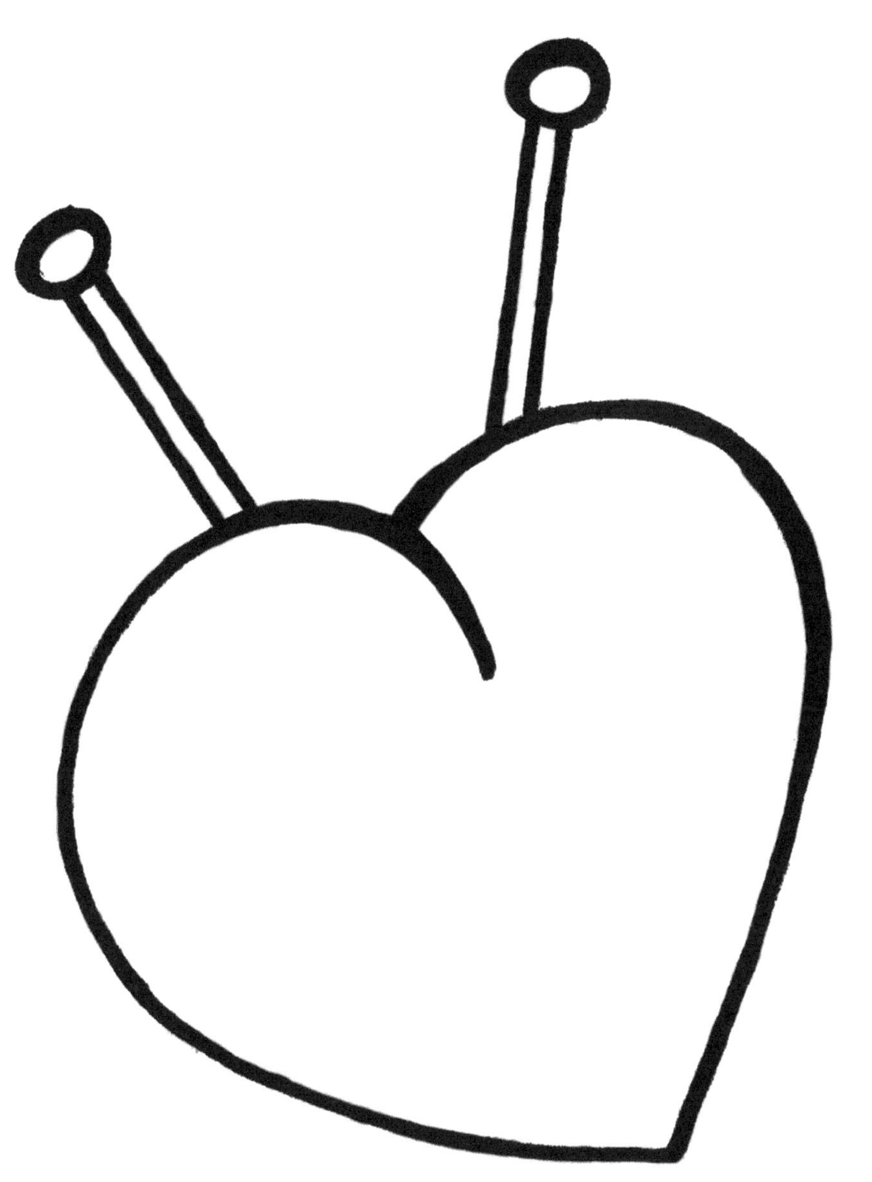

Alien Love

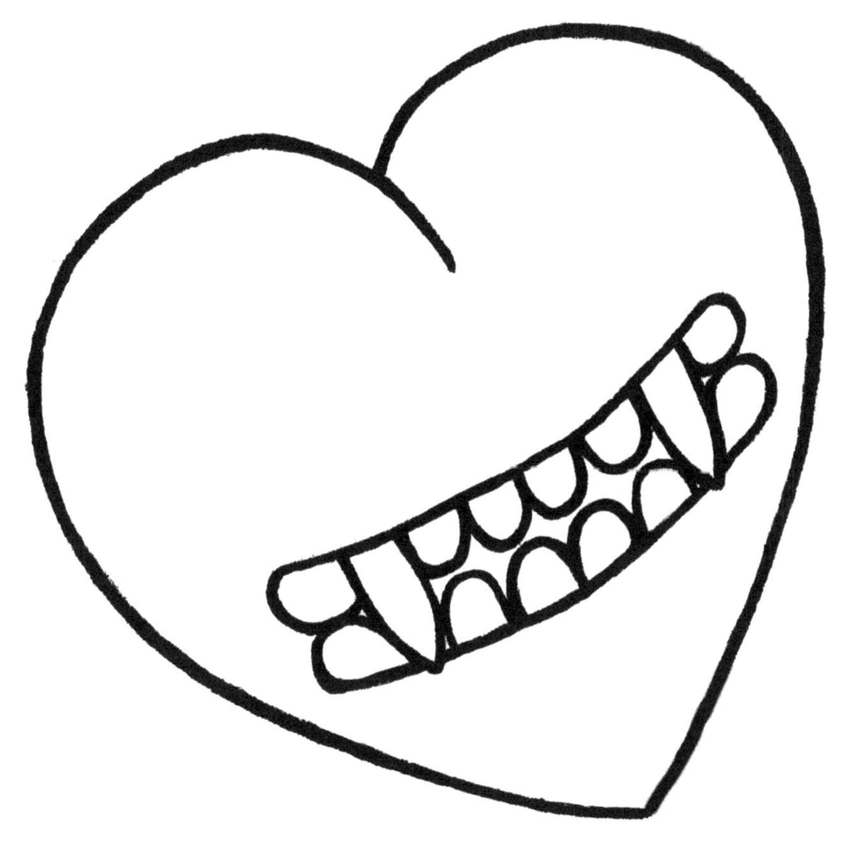

Love Sucks

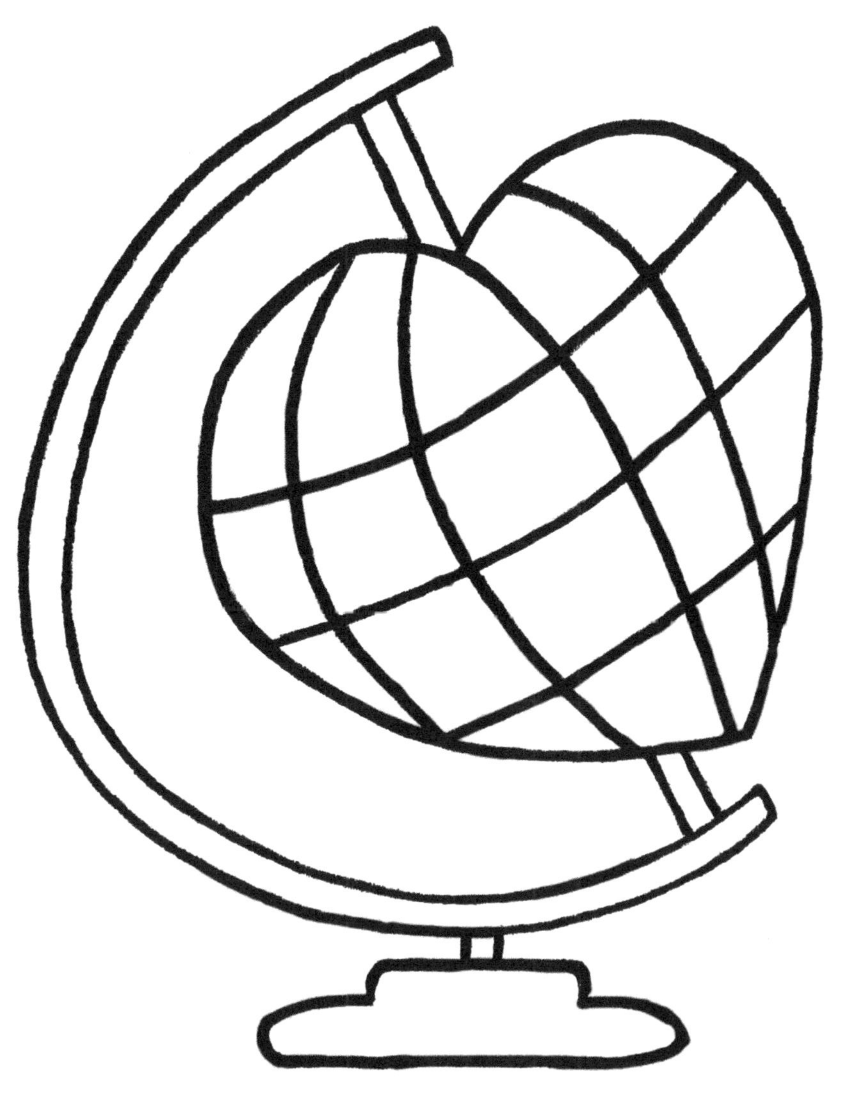

Love Makes the World Go 'Round

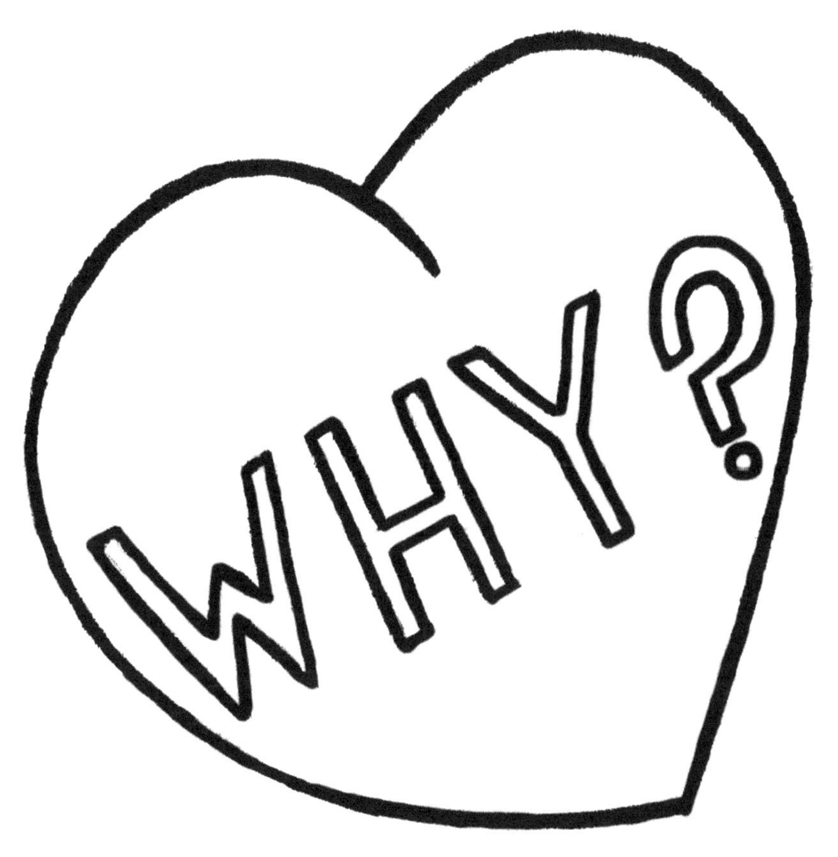

Unrequited Love

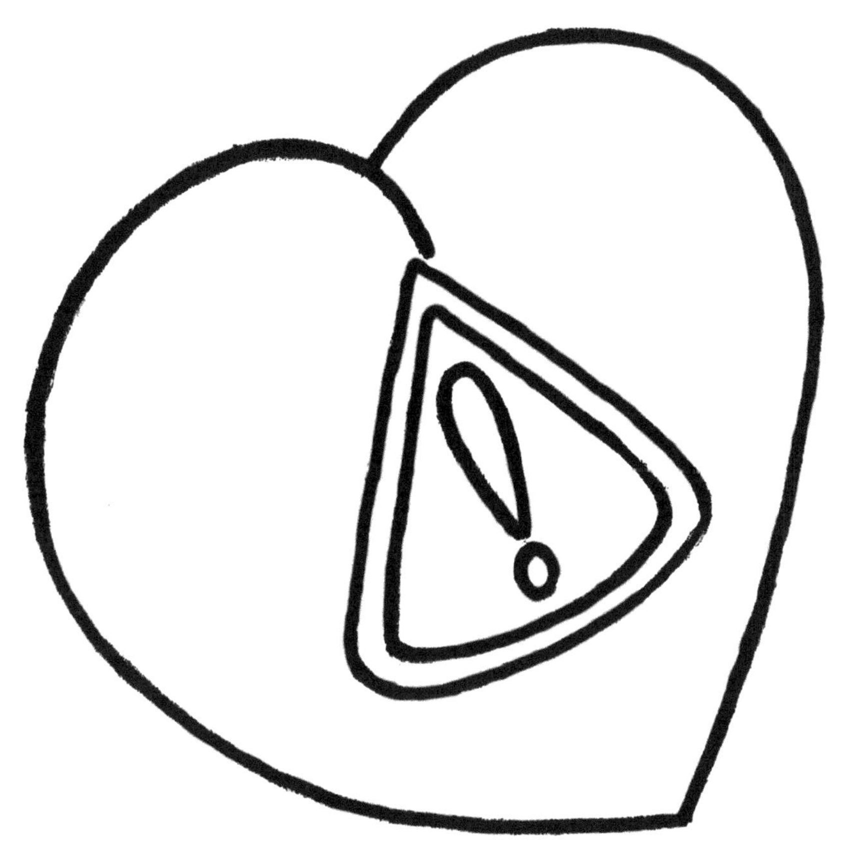

Cautious Love

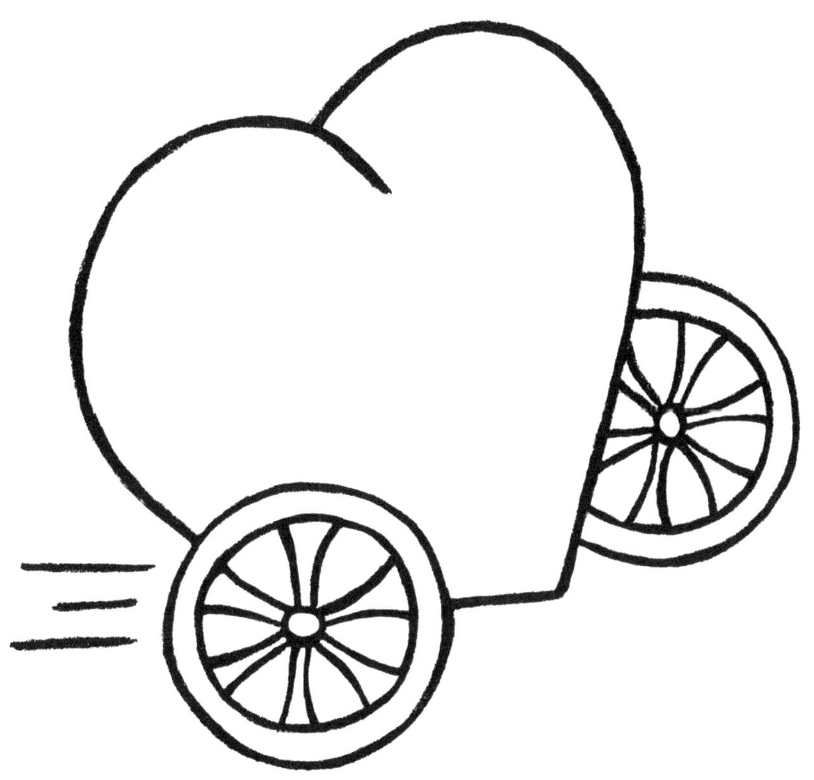

Love on Wheels

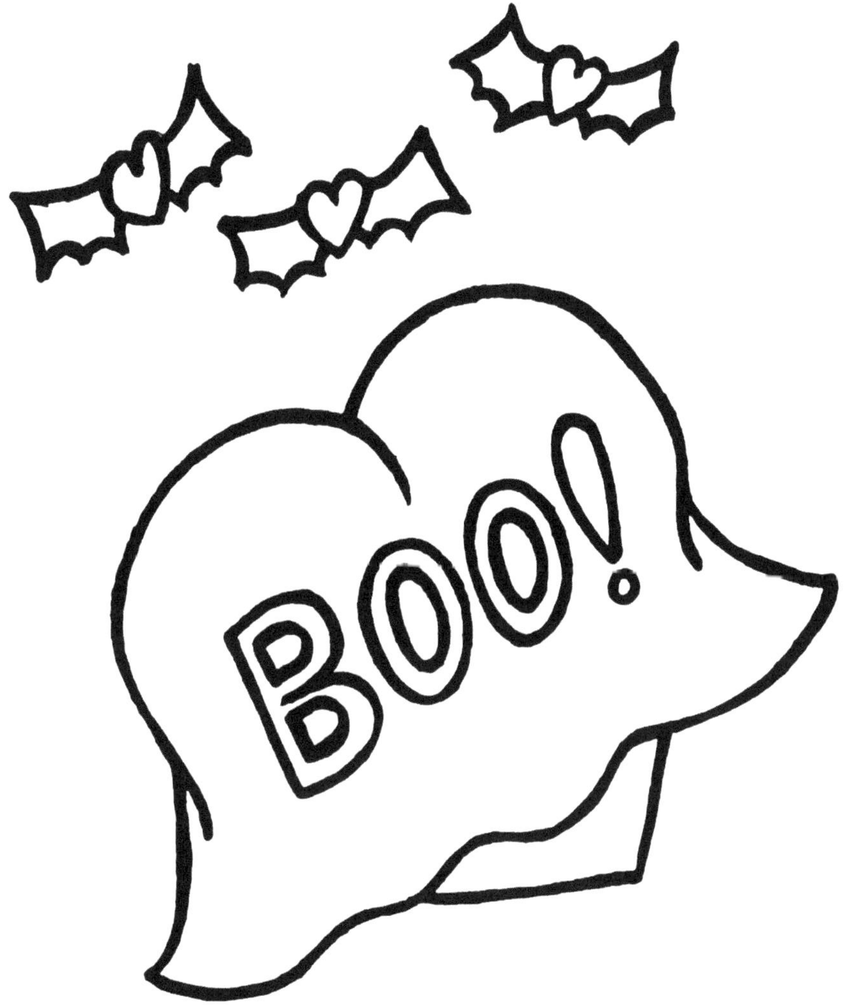

Love Fright

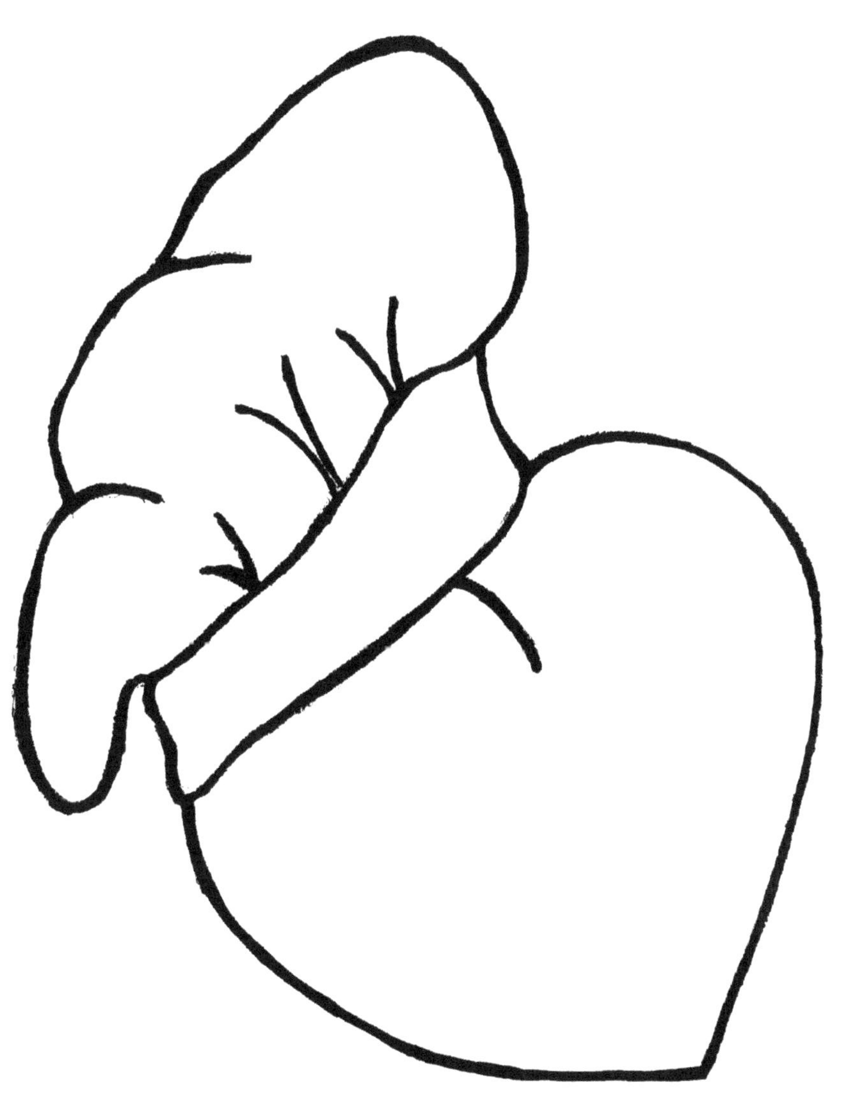

Tasty Love

Love Muffin

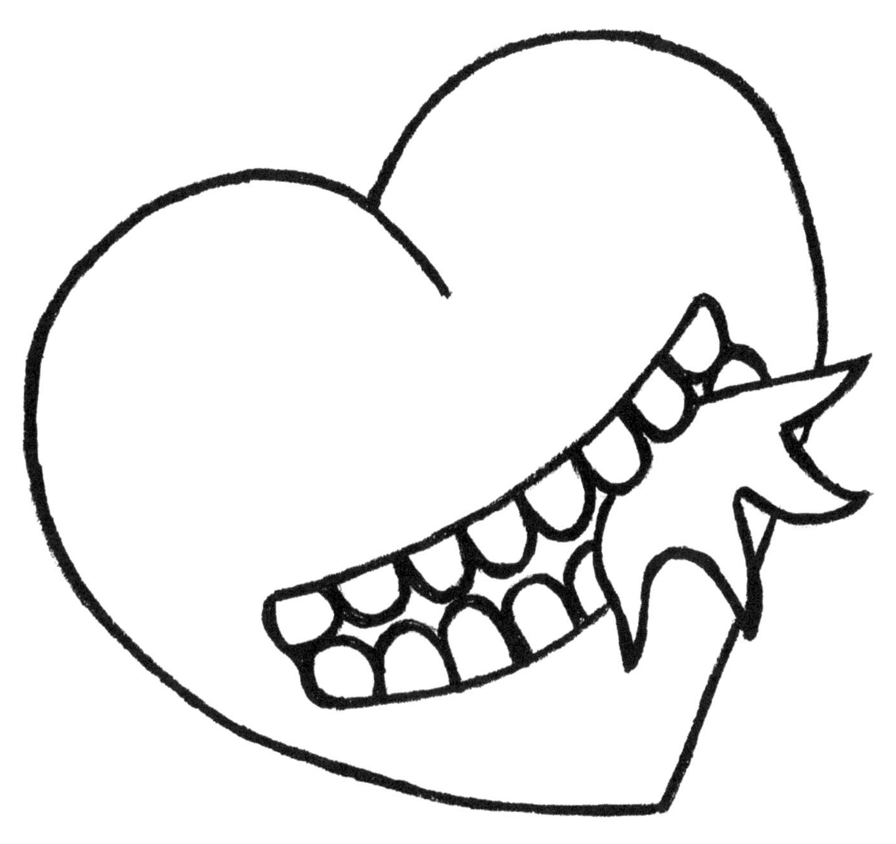

Love Bites Again

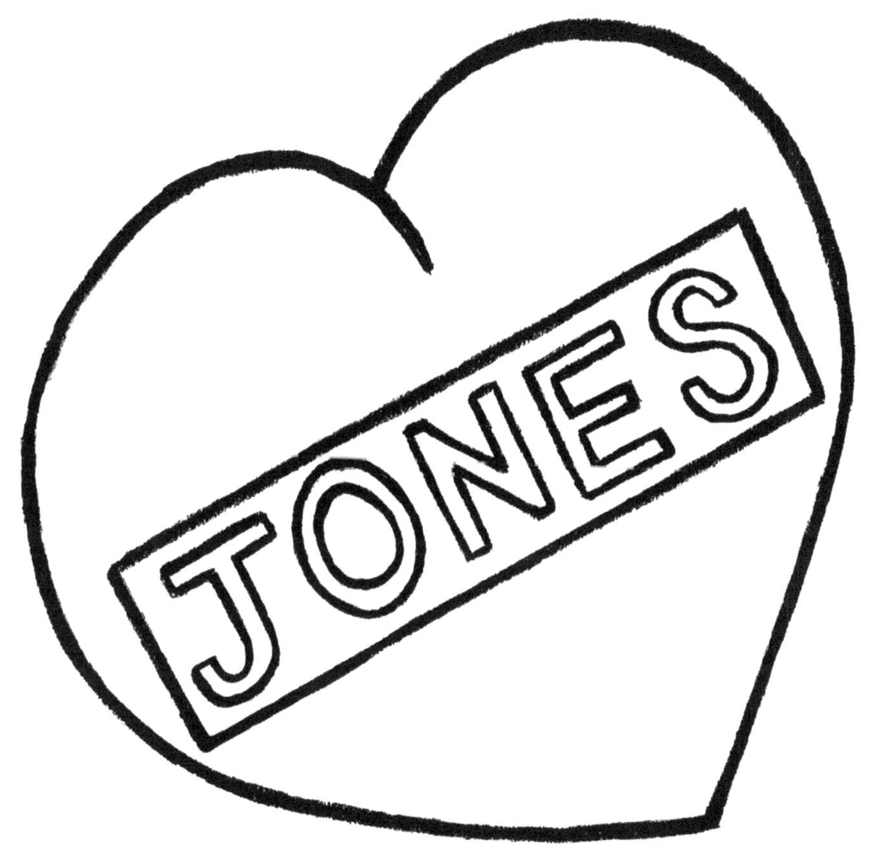

Love Jones

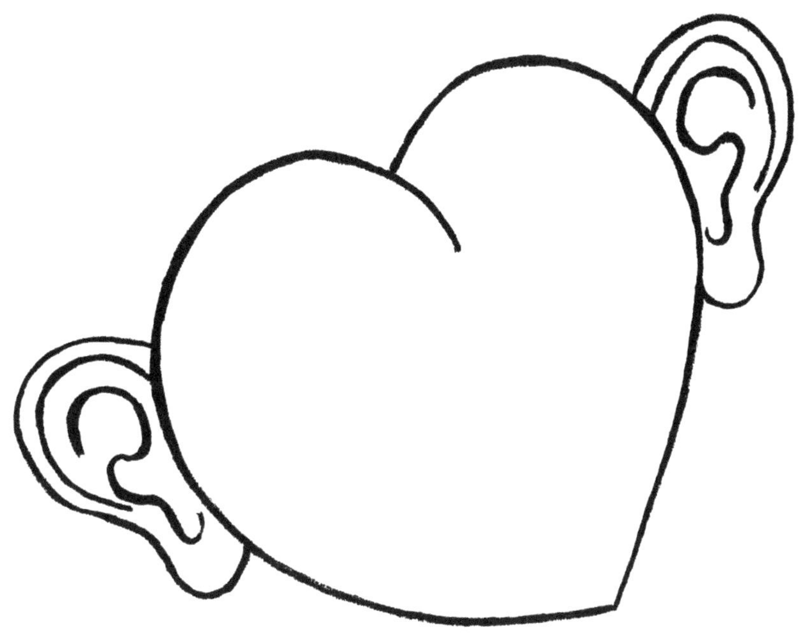

Love Listens

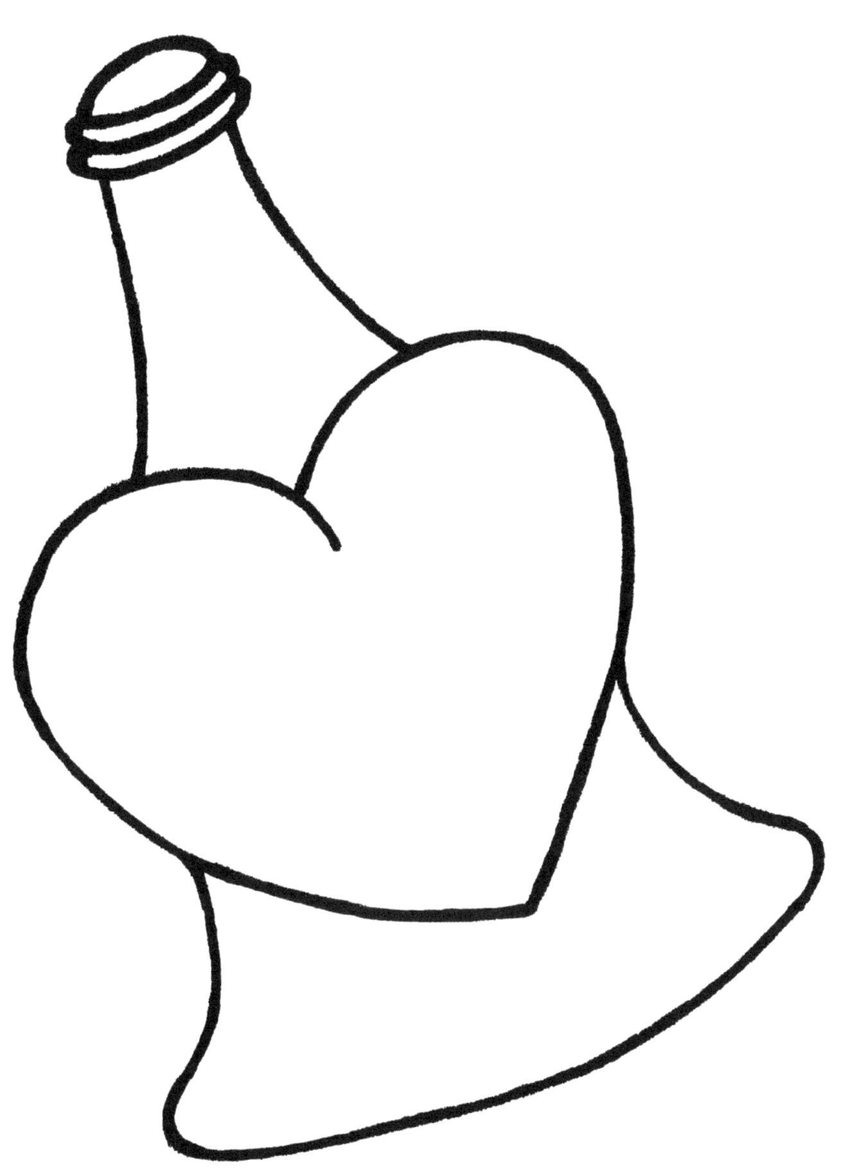

Love Potion

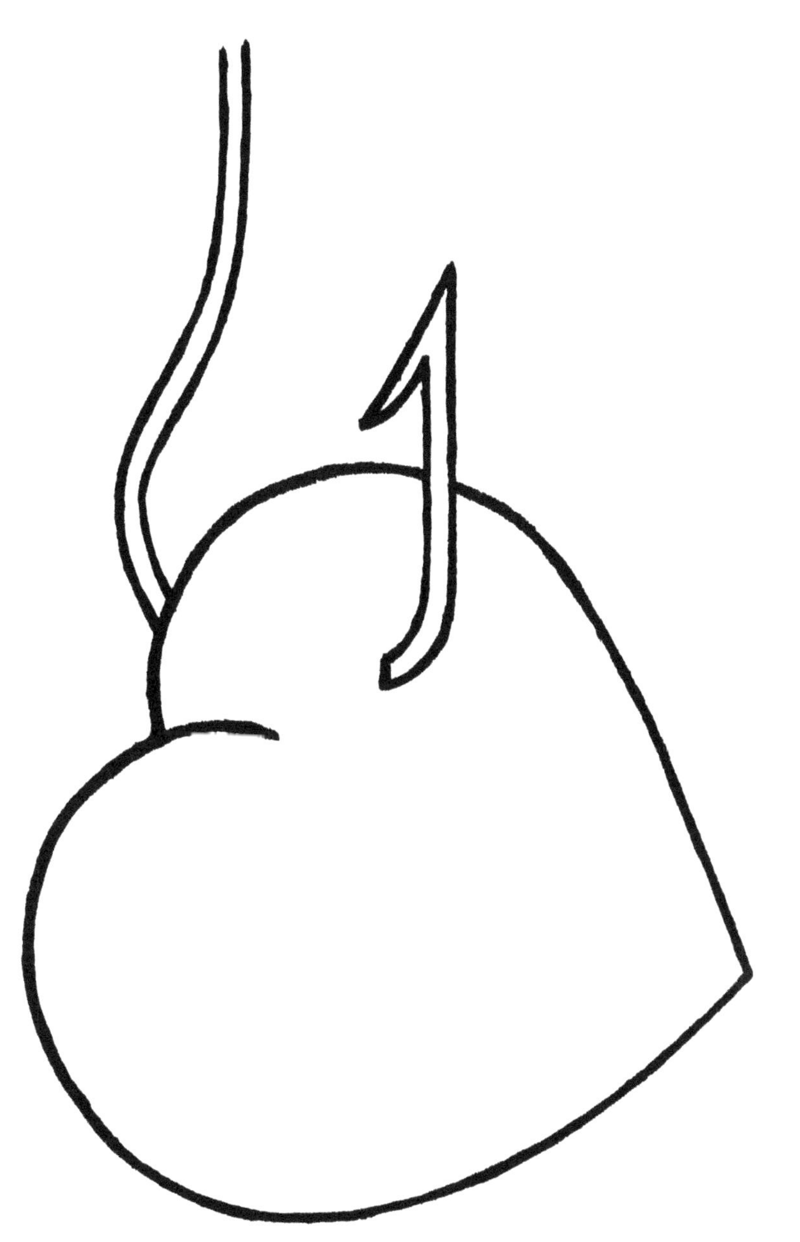

Hooked on Love

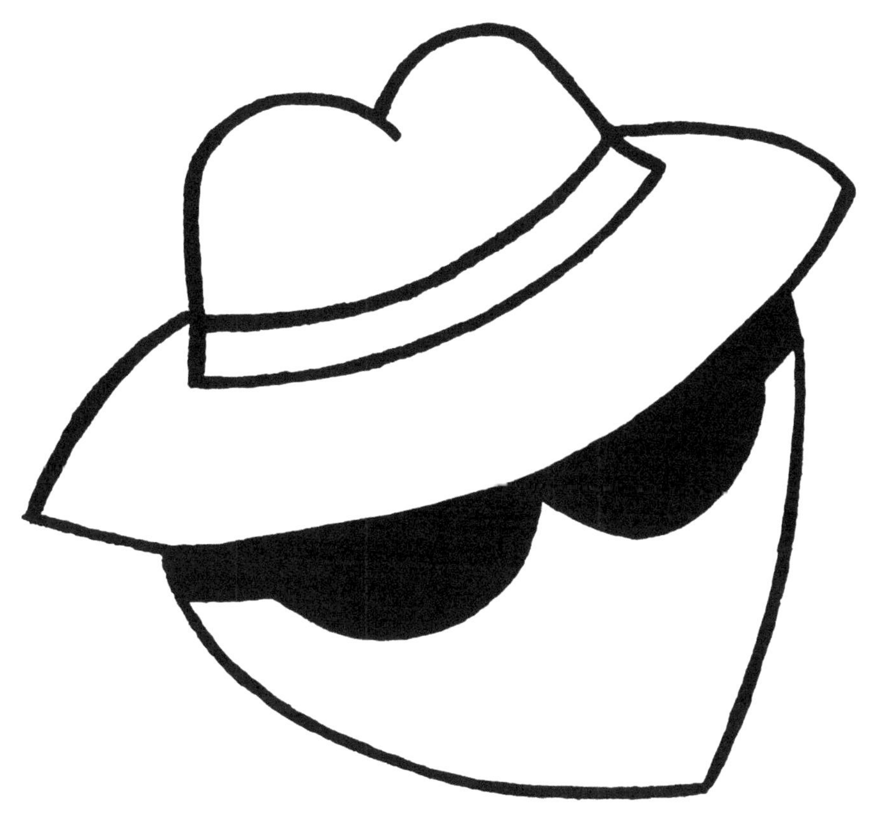

Secret Love

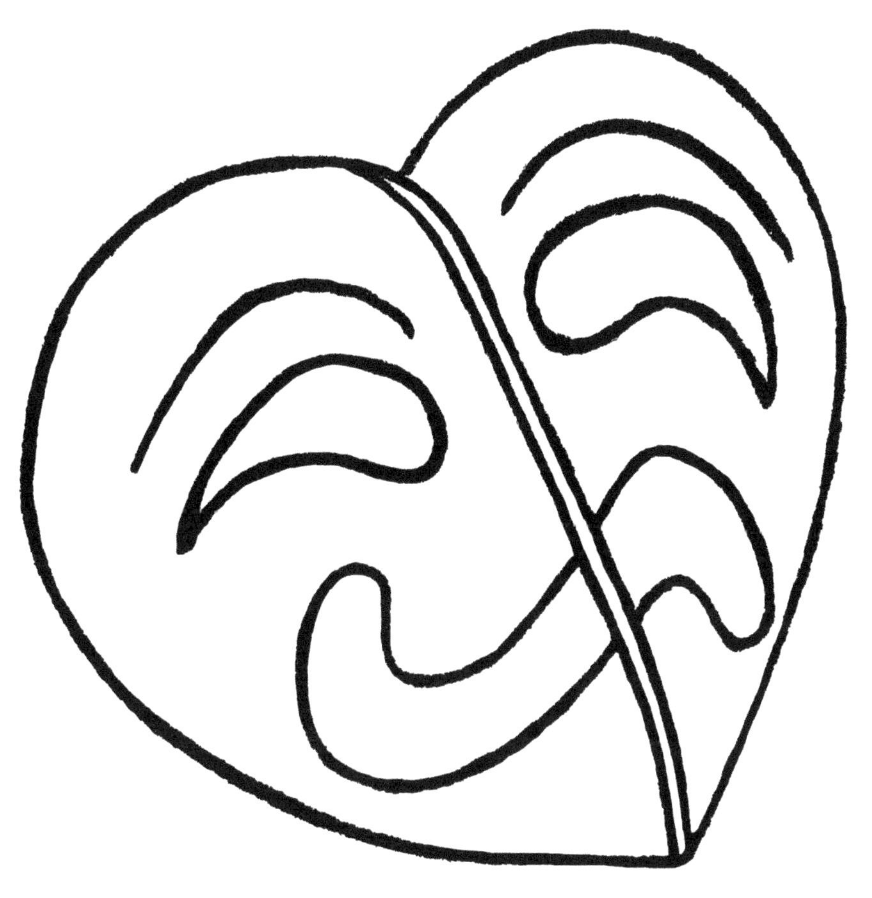

Two Faces of Love

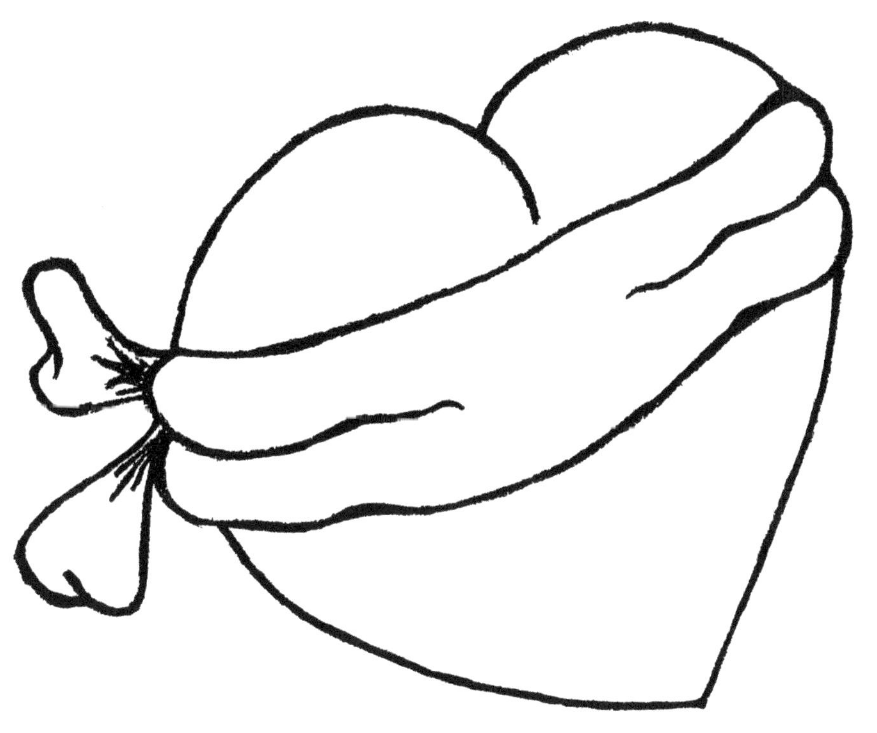

Blinded by Love

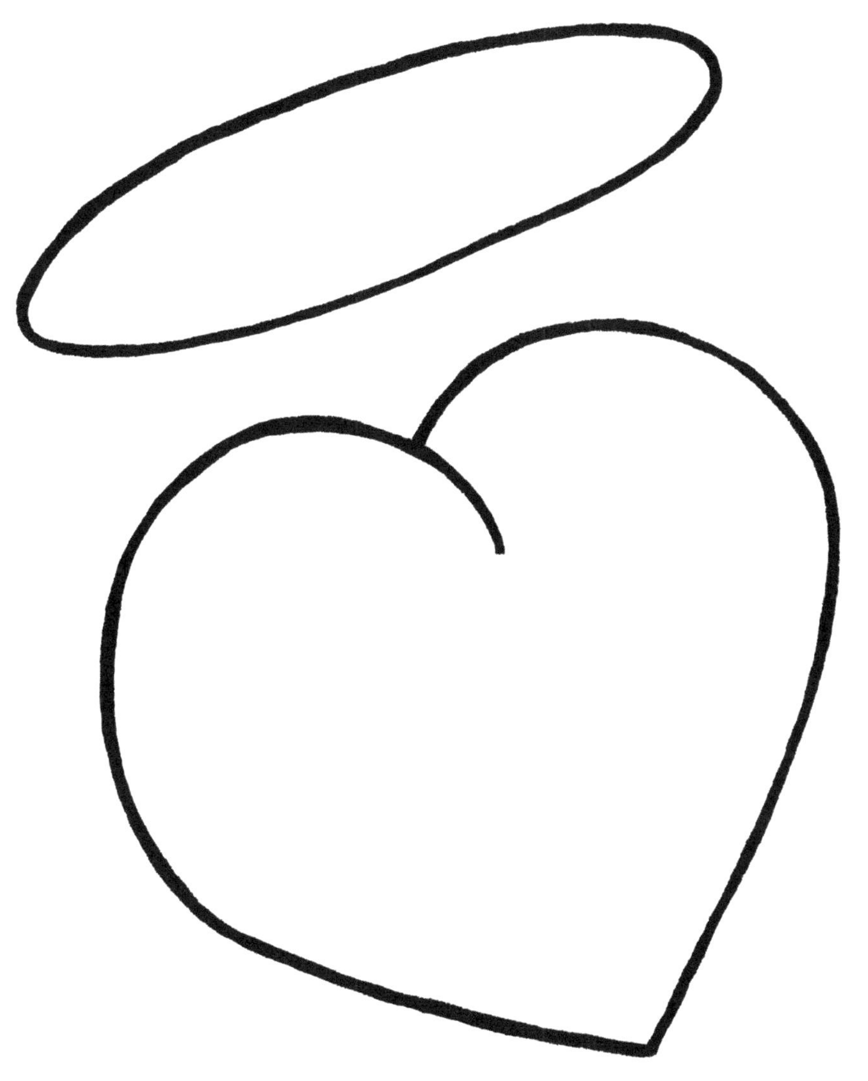

Heavenly Love

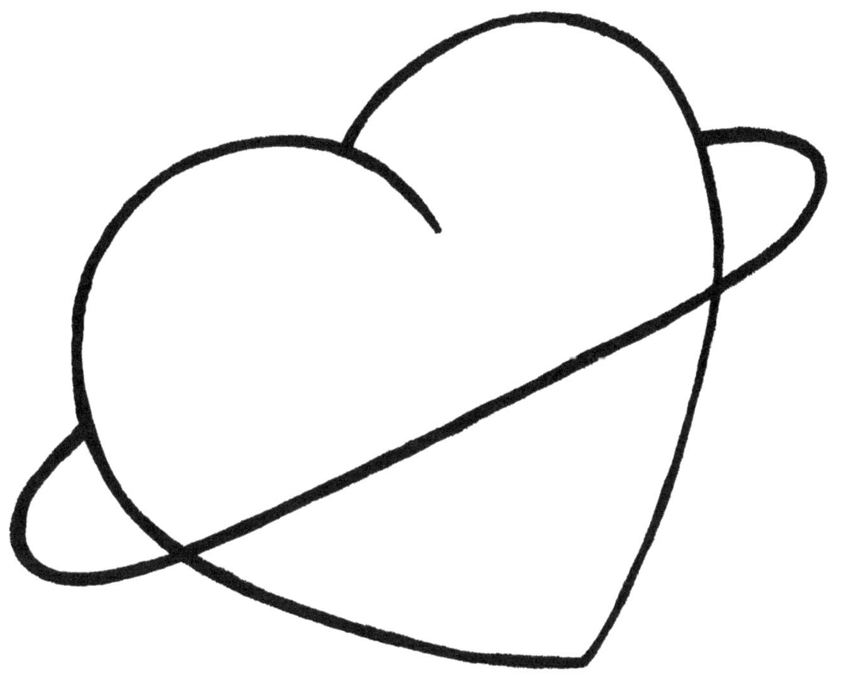

Circle of Love

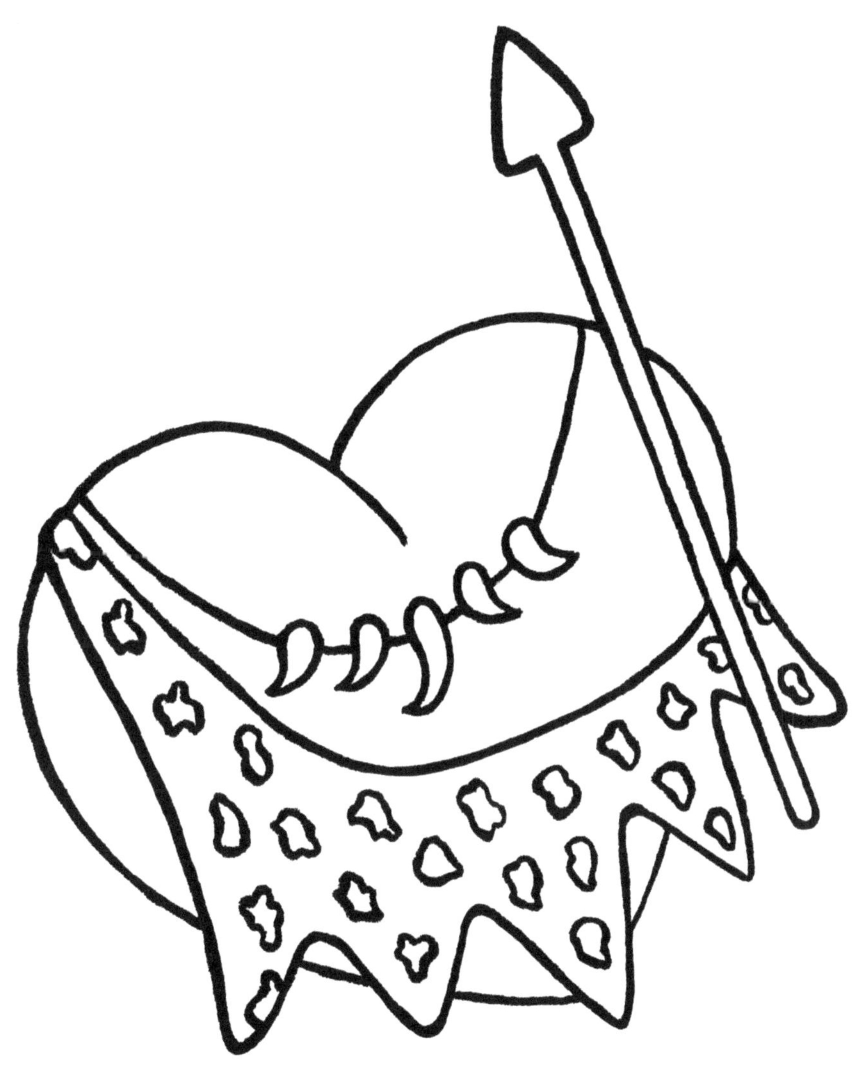

Wild Love

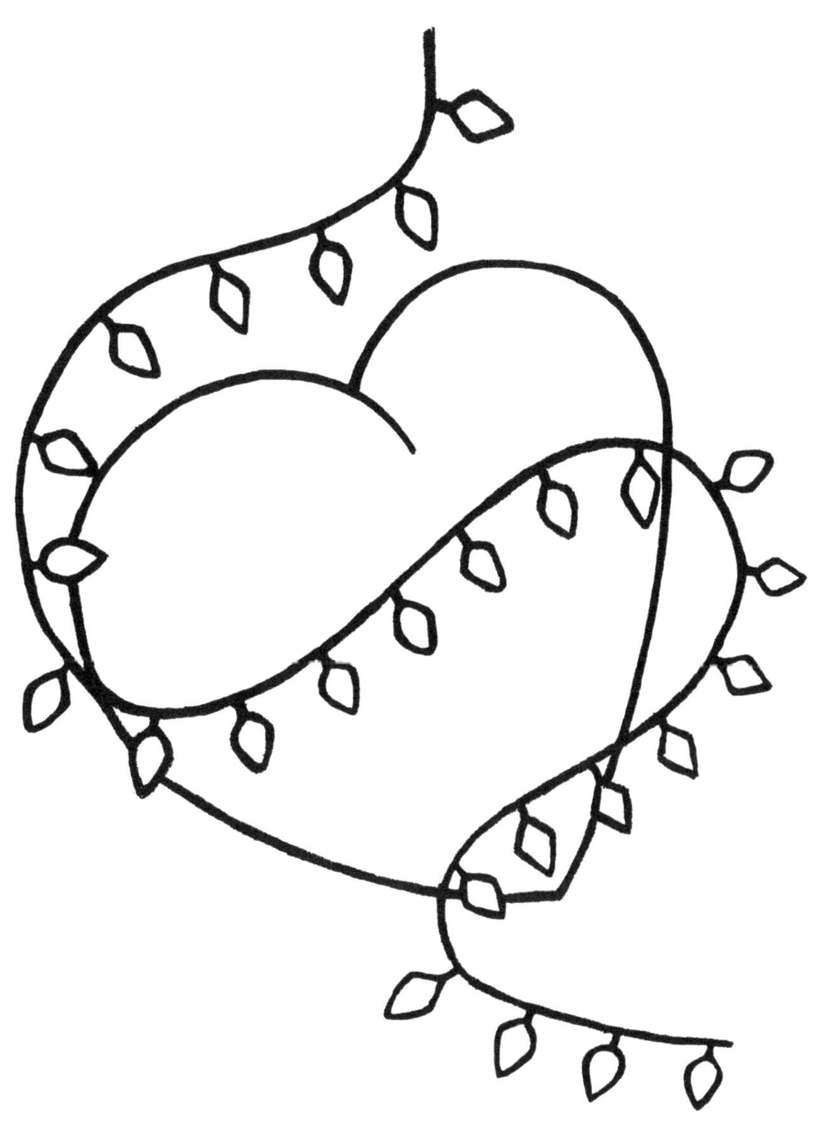

Holiday Love

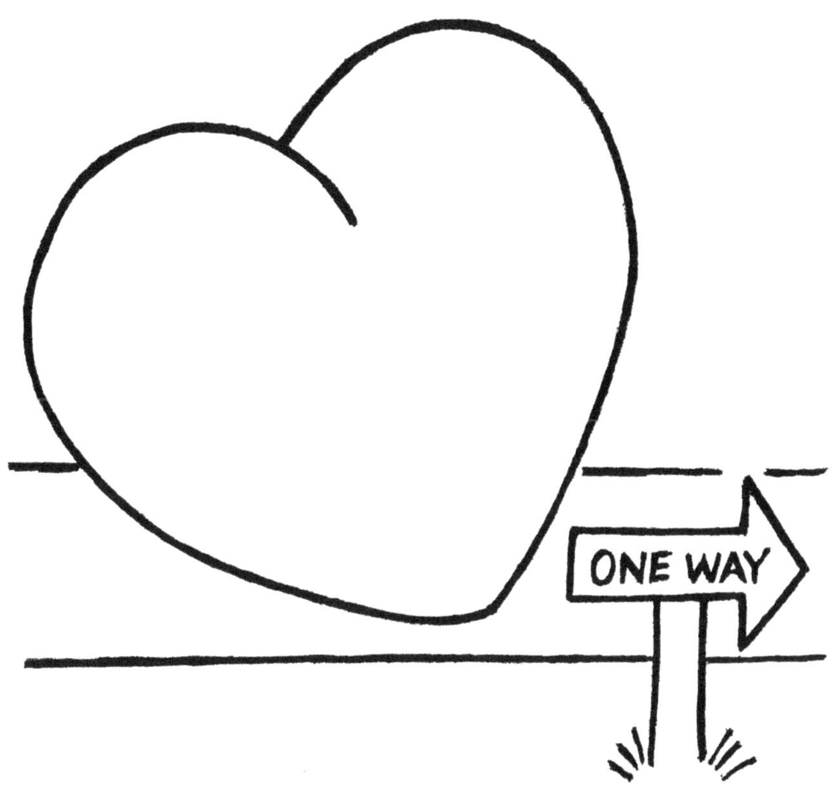

One-Way Love

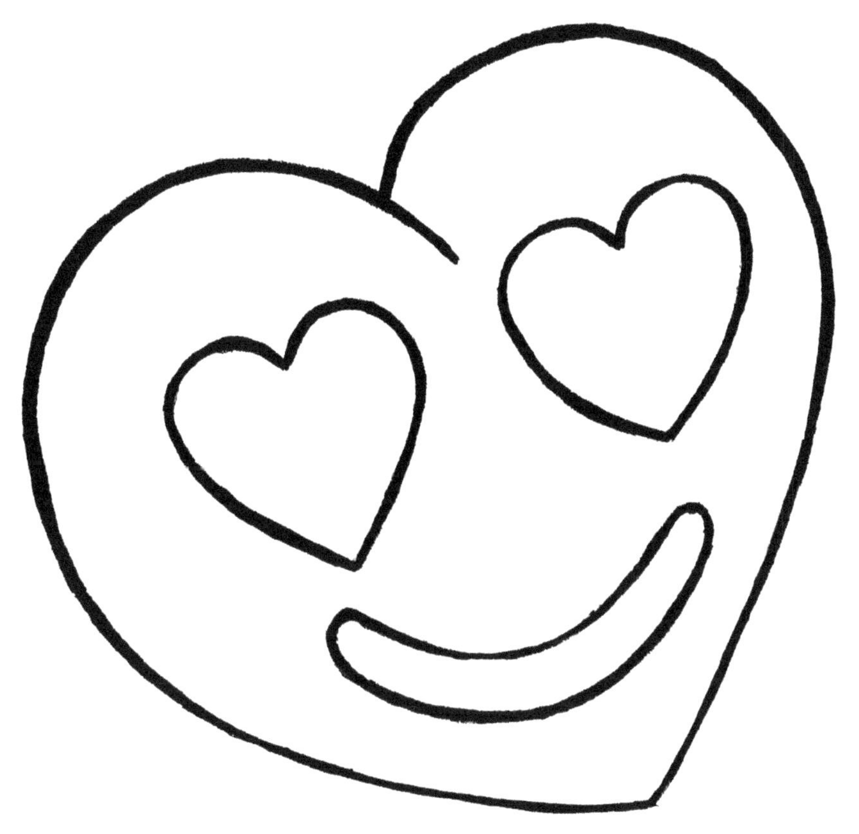

Emoji Love

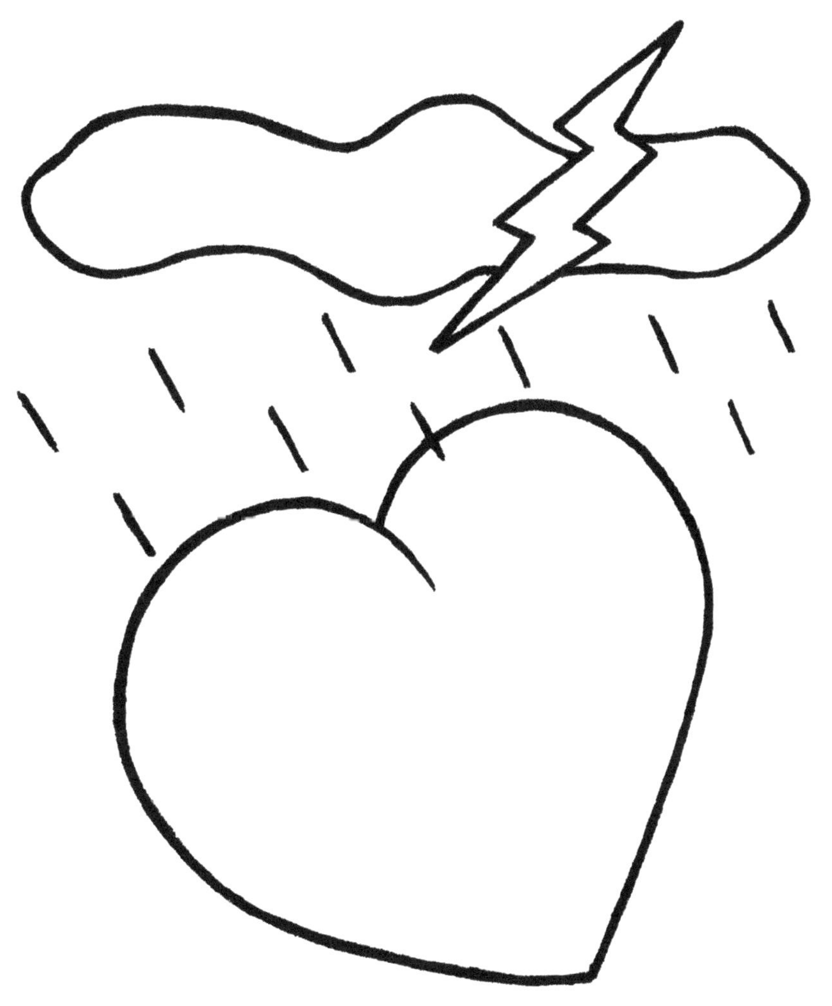

Stormy Love

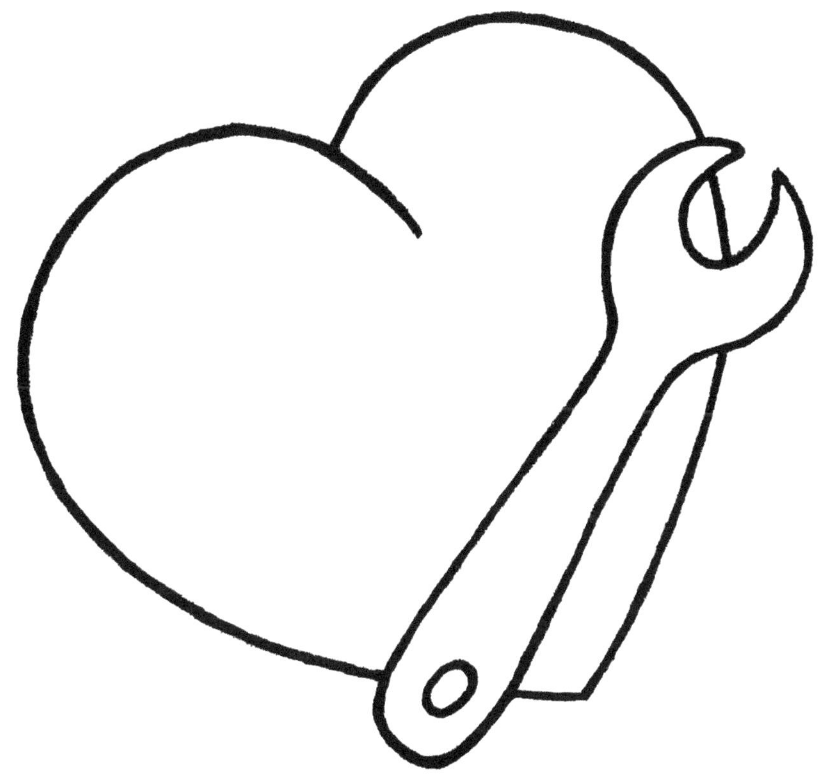

Love Fix

Love Is the Answer

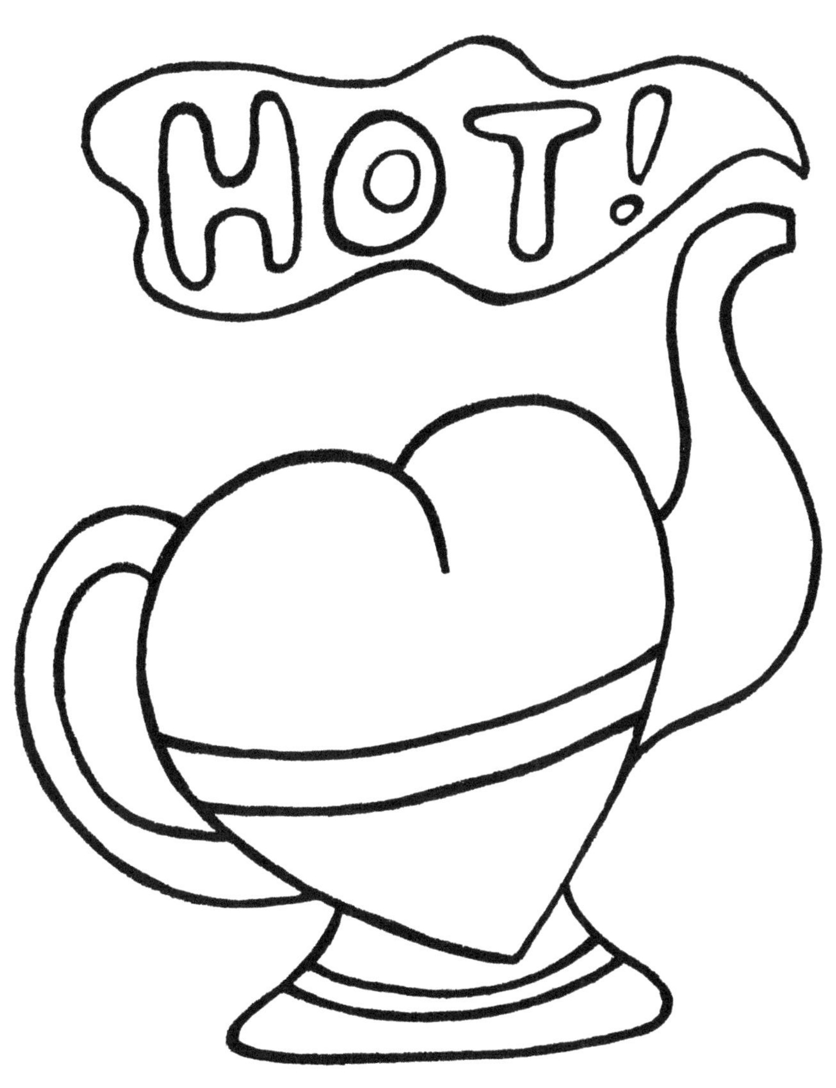

Steamy Love

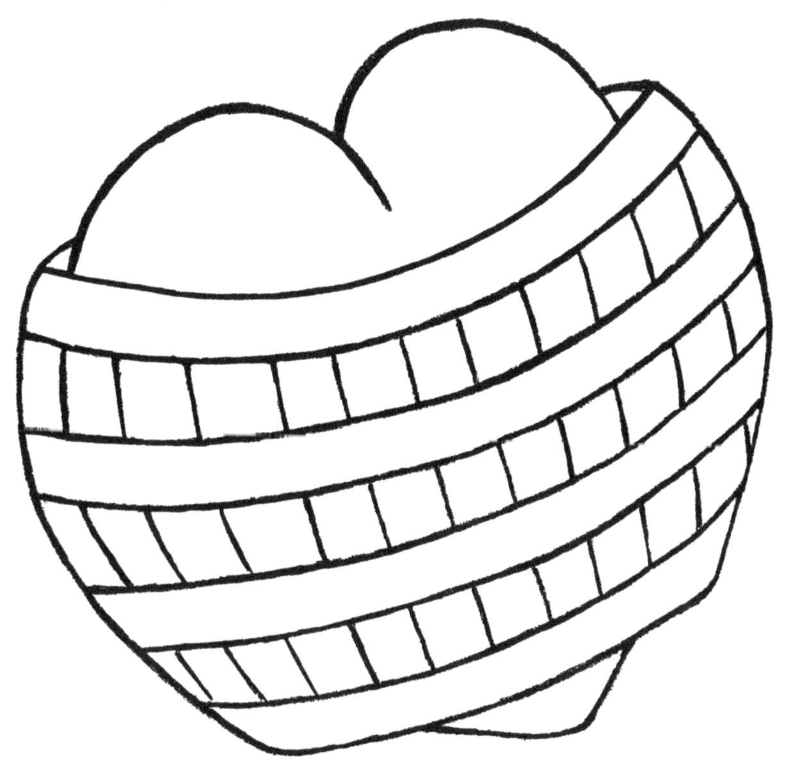

Love in a Barrel

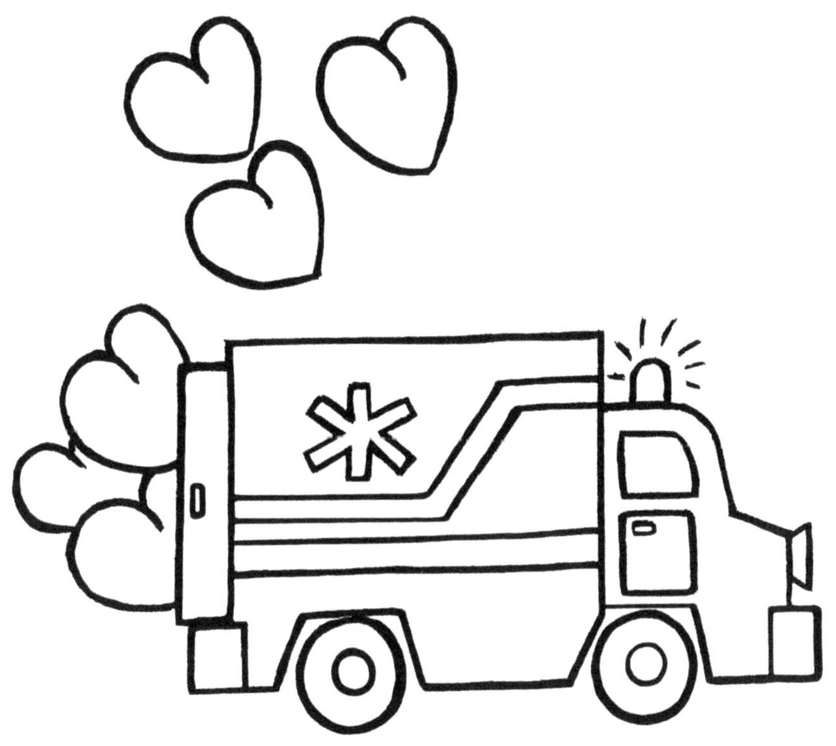

Love Emergency

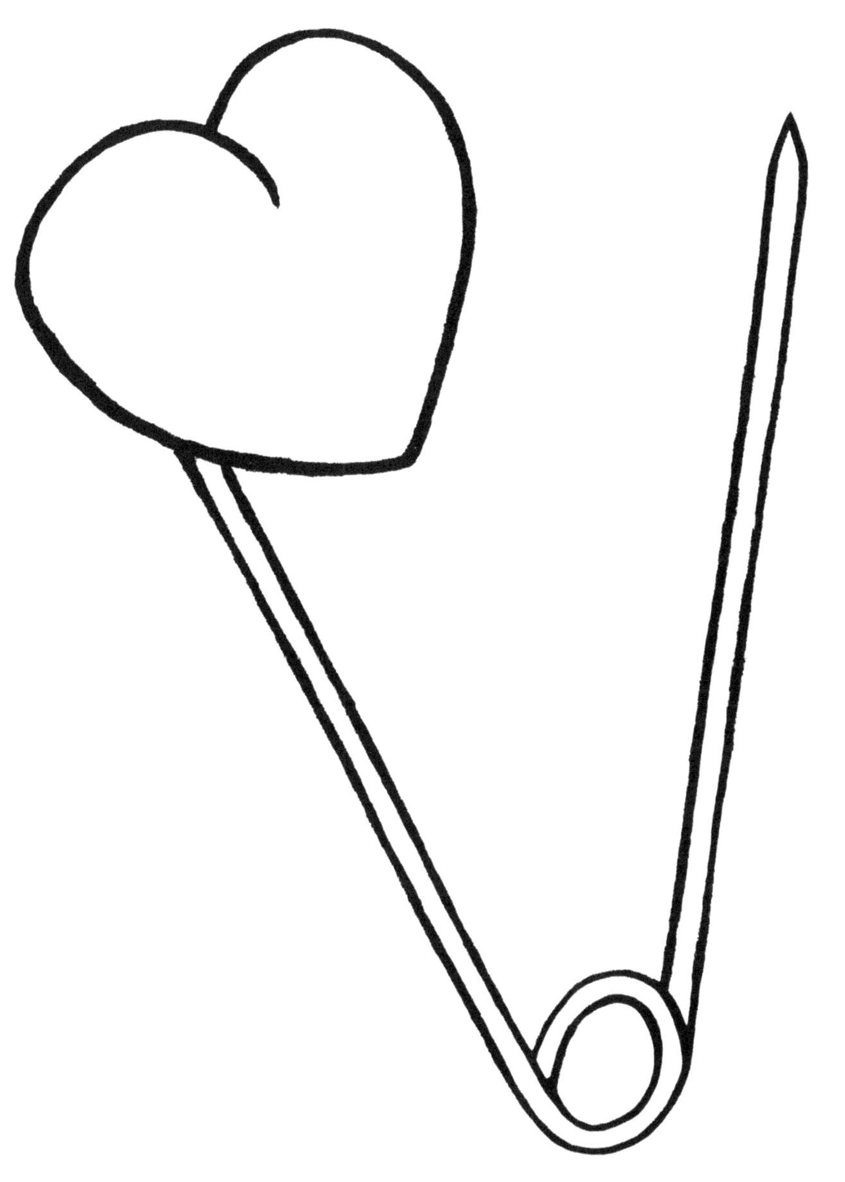

Safe Love

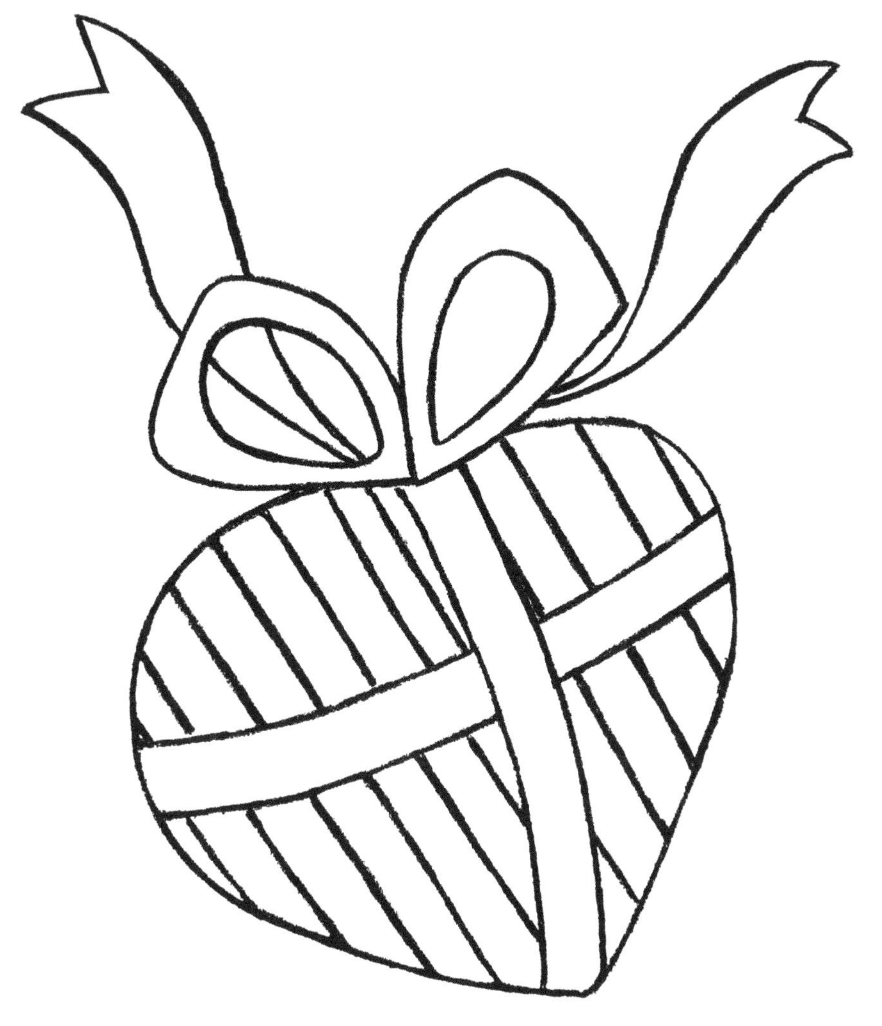

Gift of Love

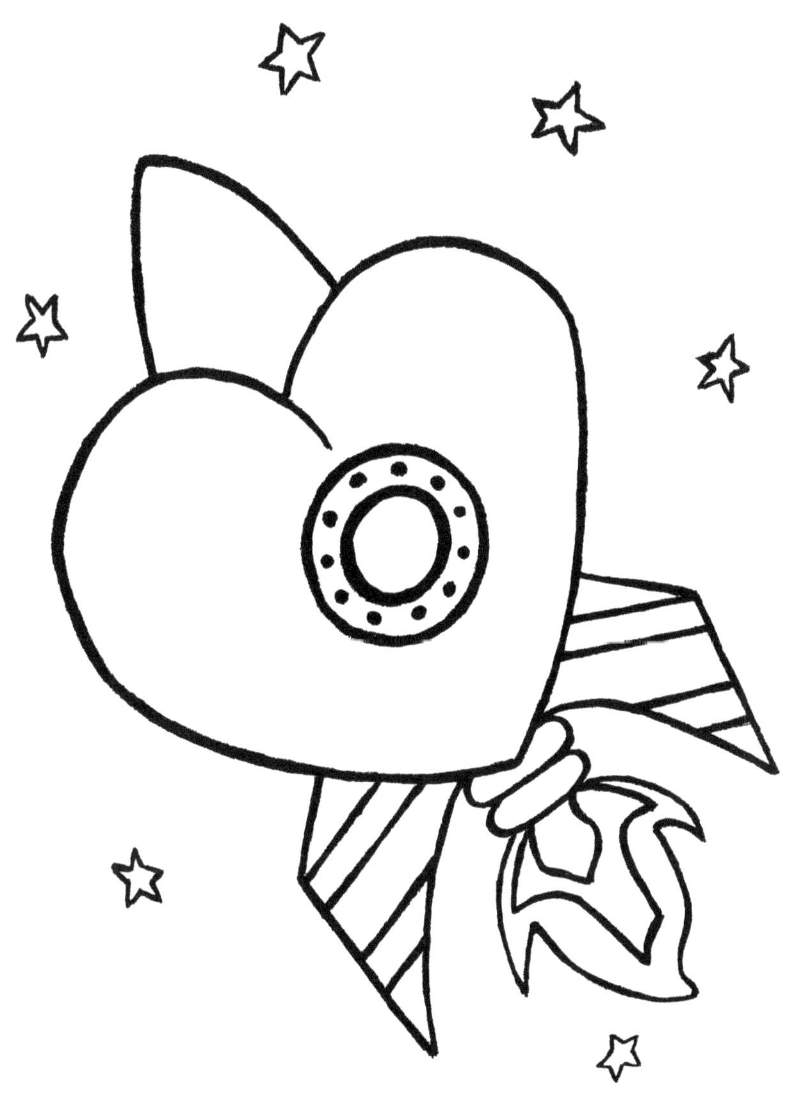

Love Like a Rocket

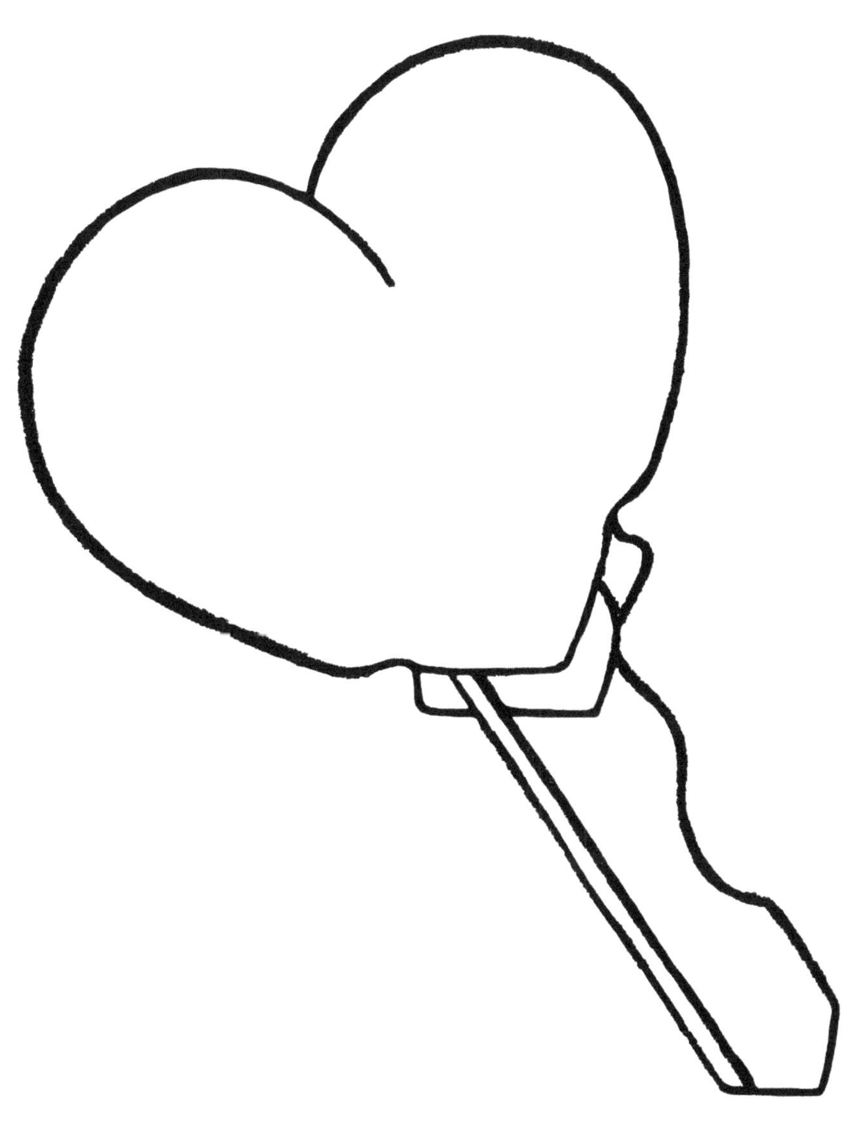

Love is the Key

Love on the Beach

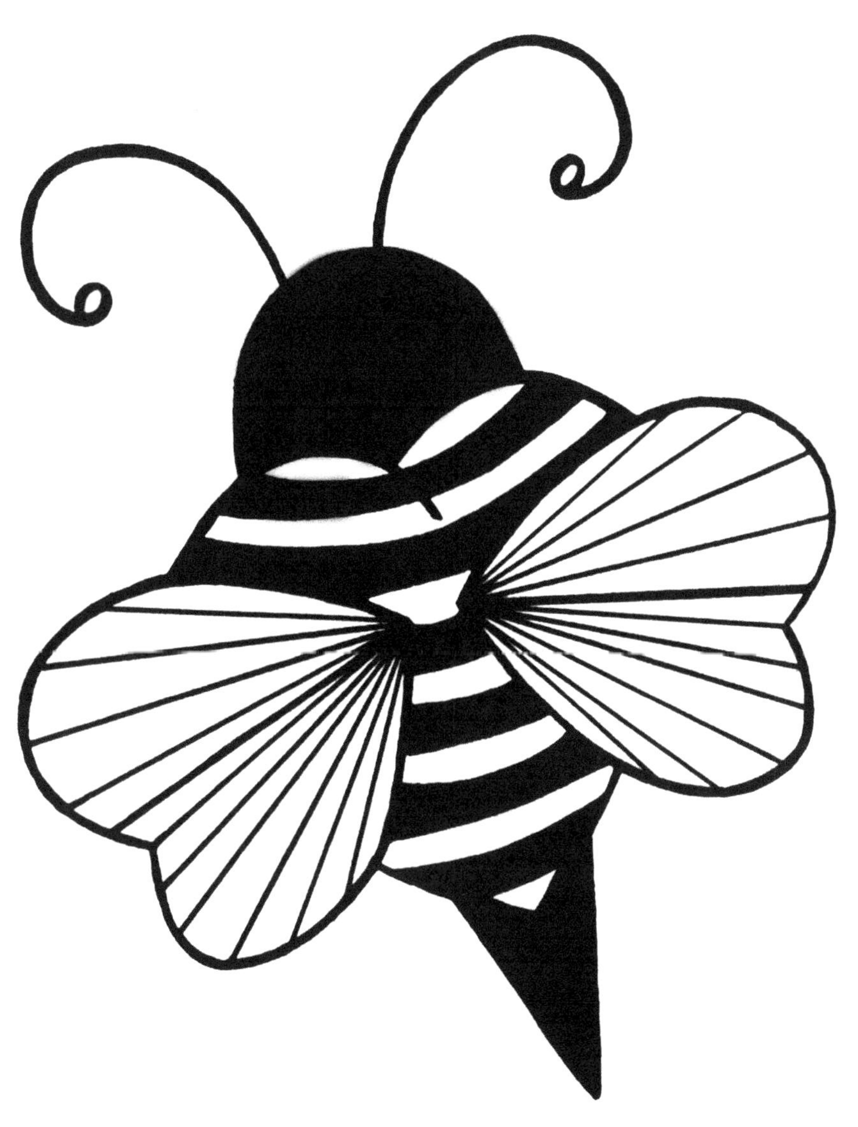

Bee-loved

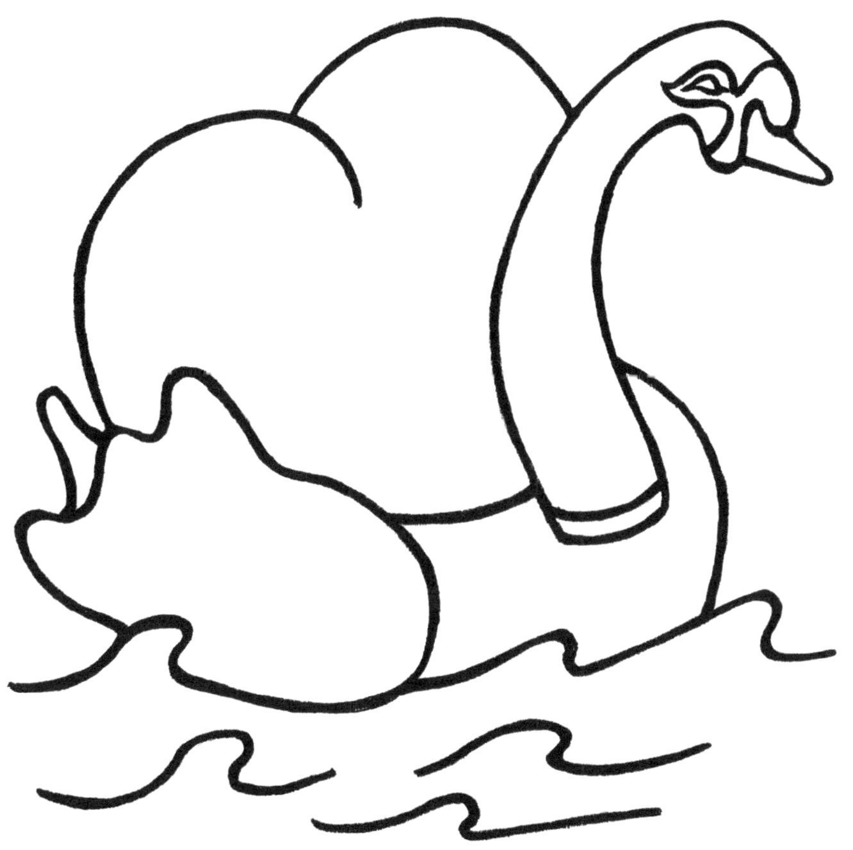

Love Floats

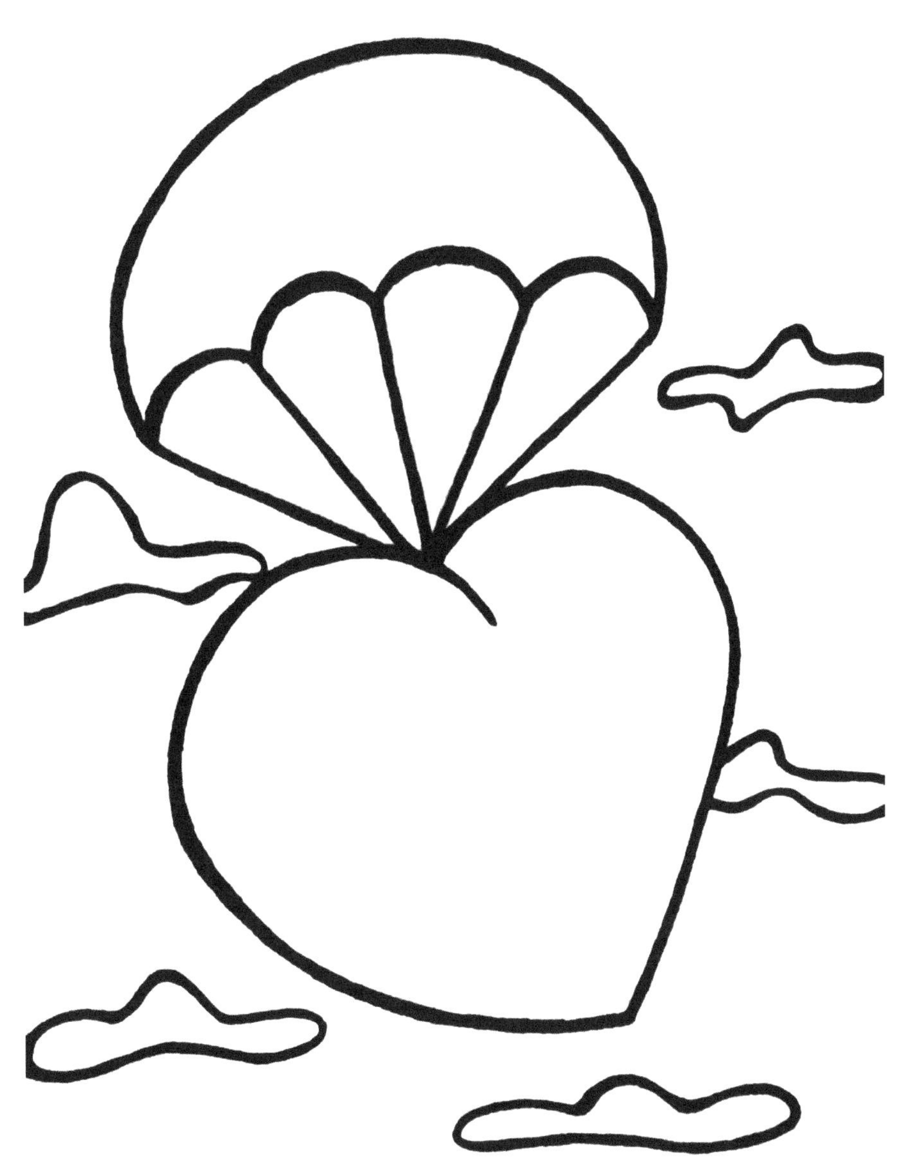

Sky-High Love

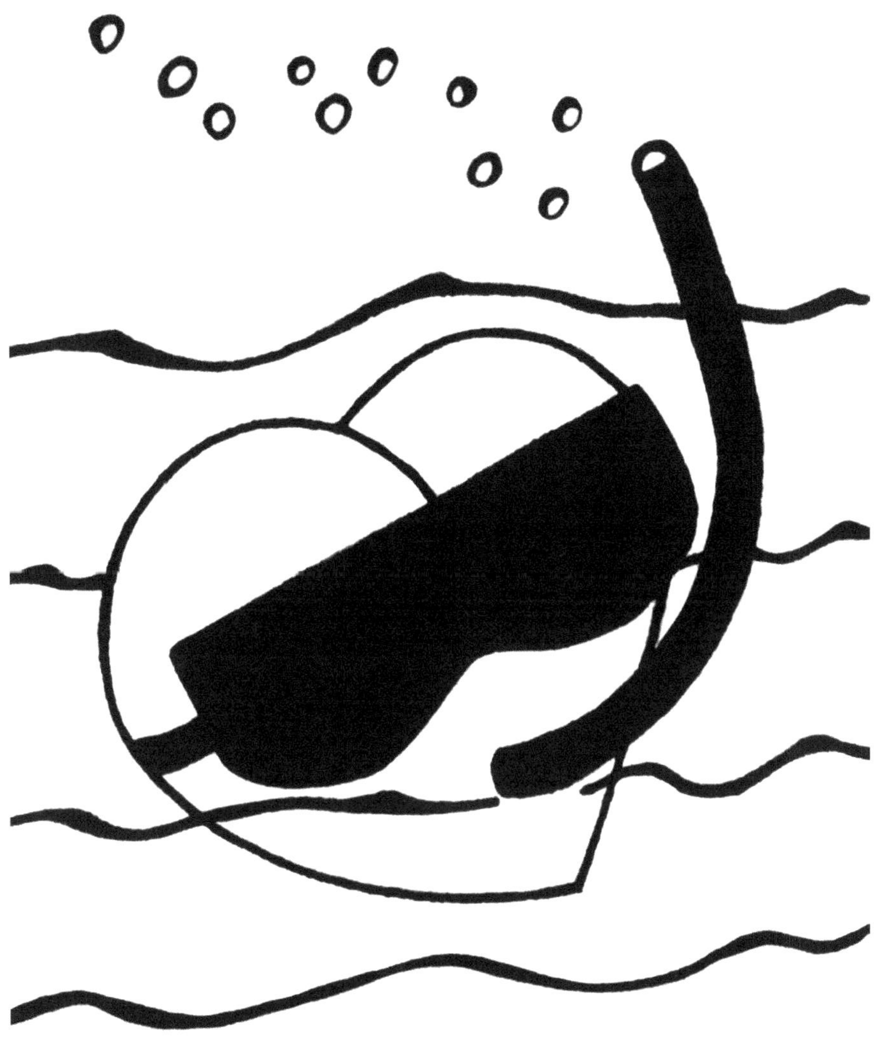

Deep Love

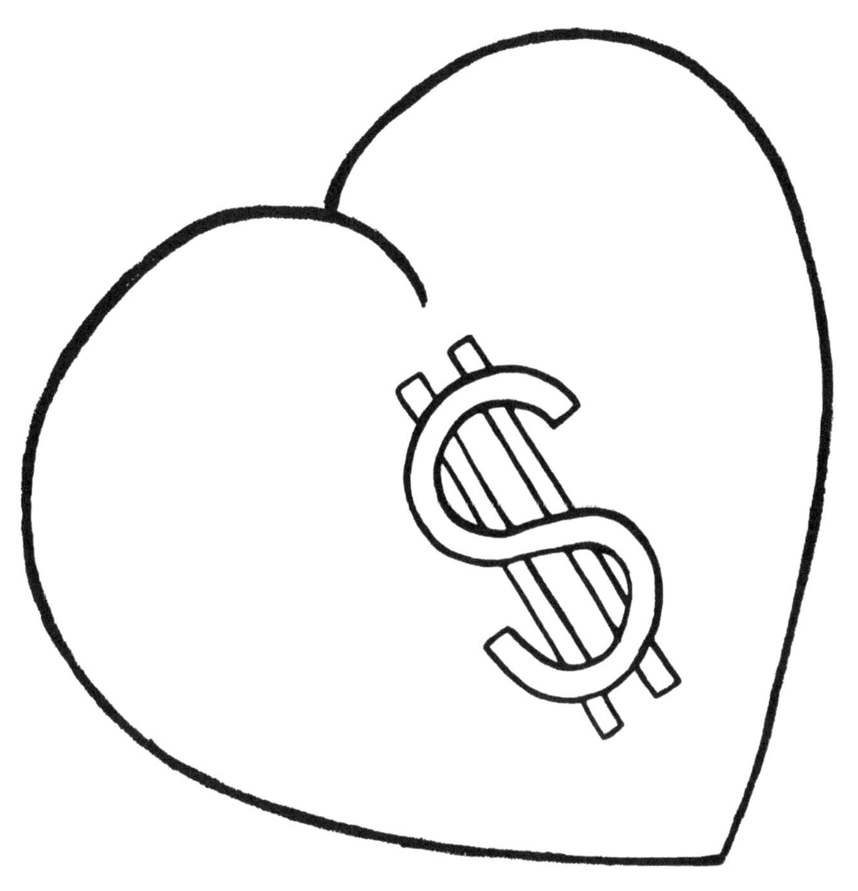

Love on the Money

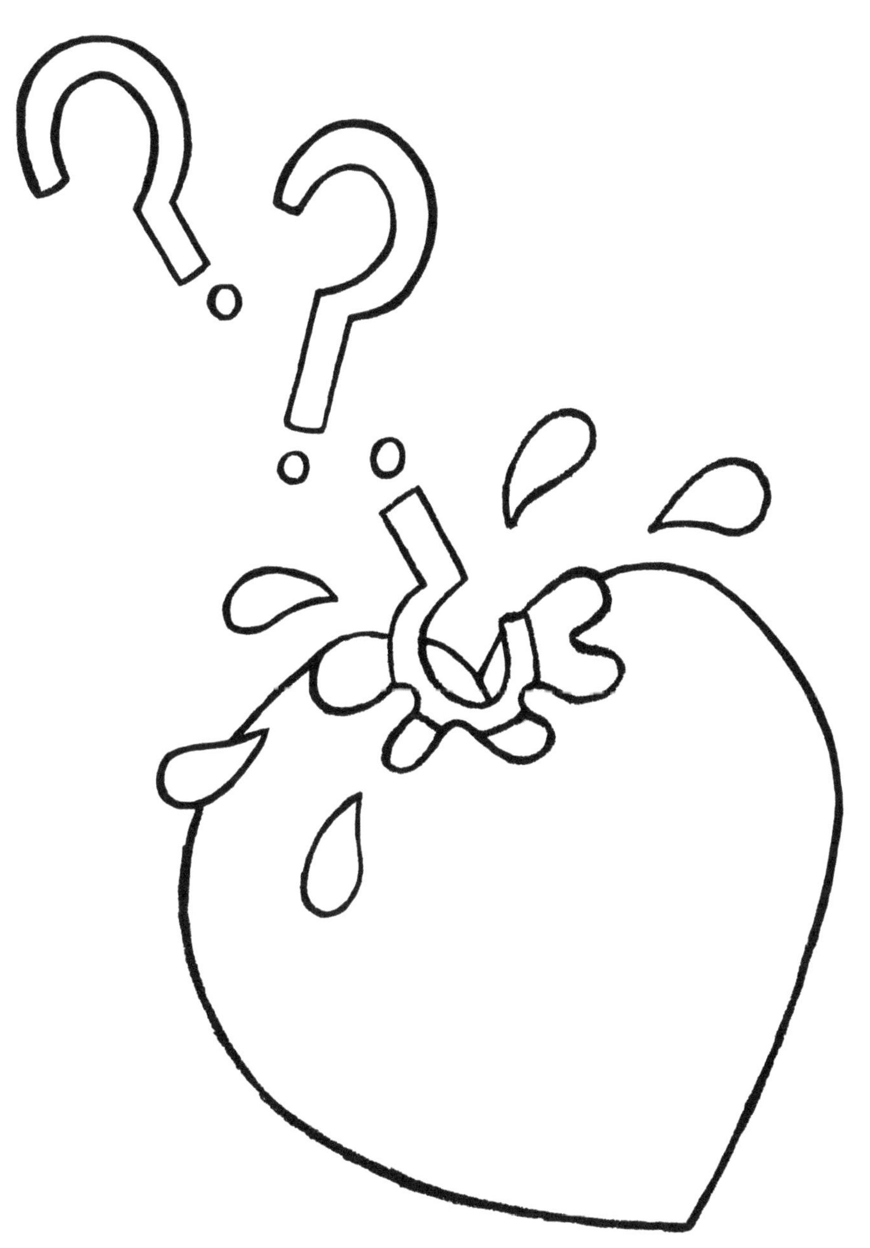

Falling in Love

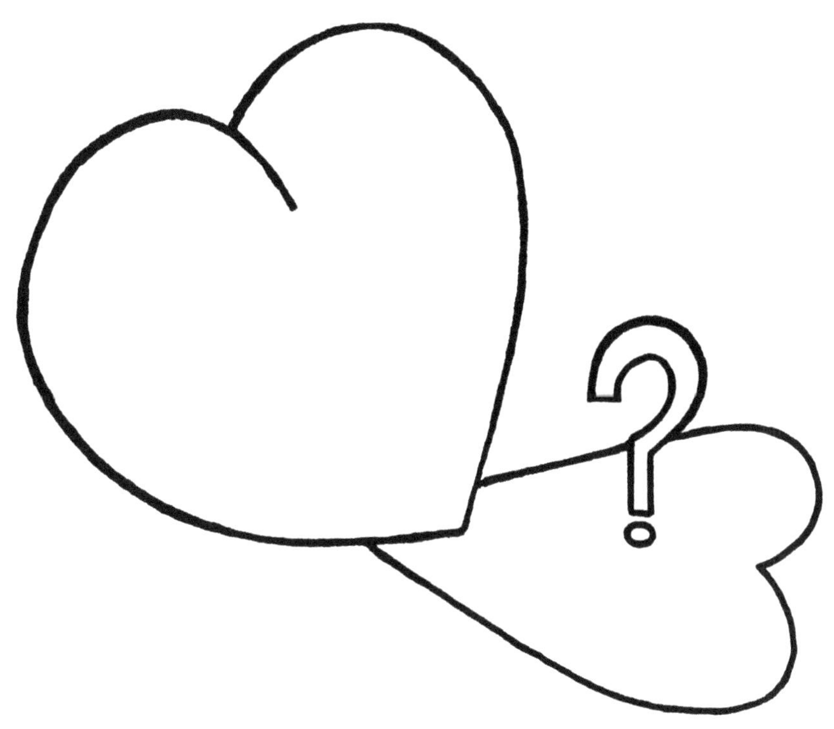

In the Shadow of Love

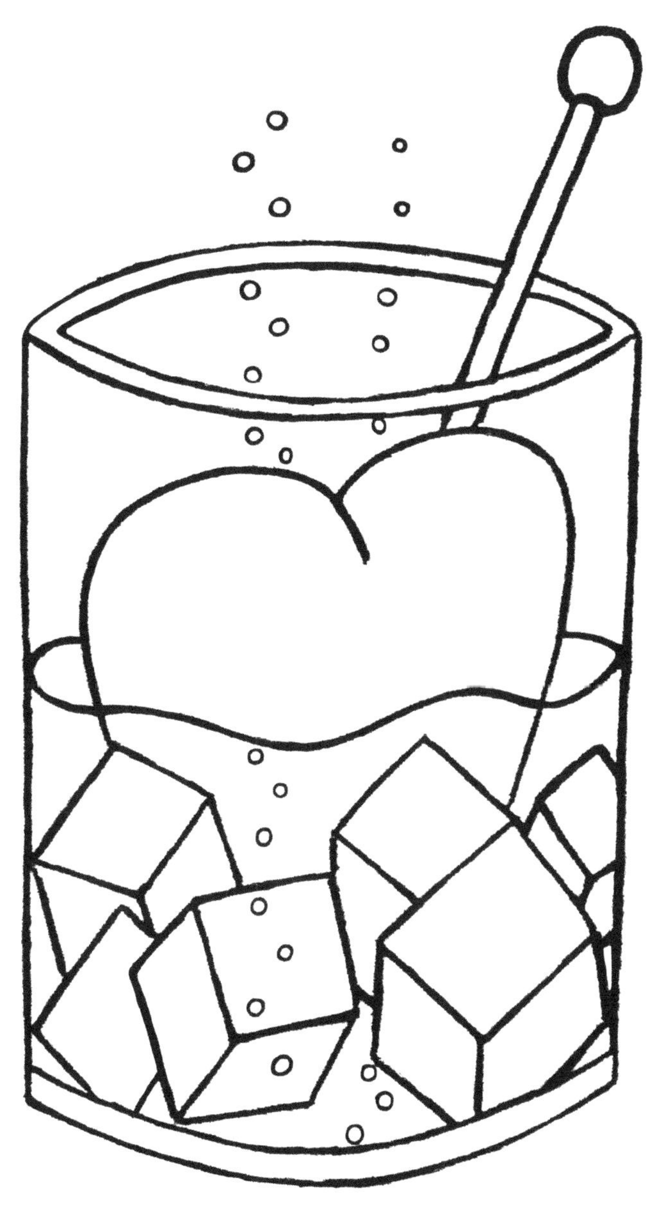

Love on the Rocks

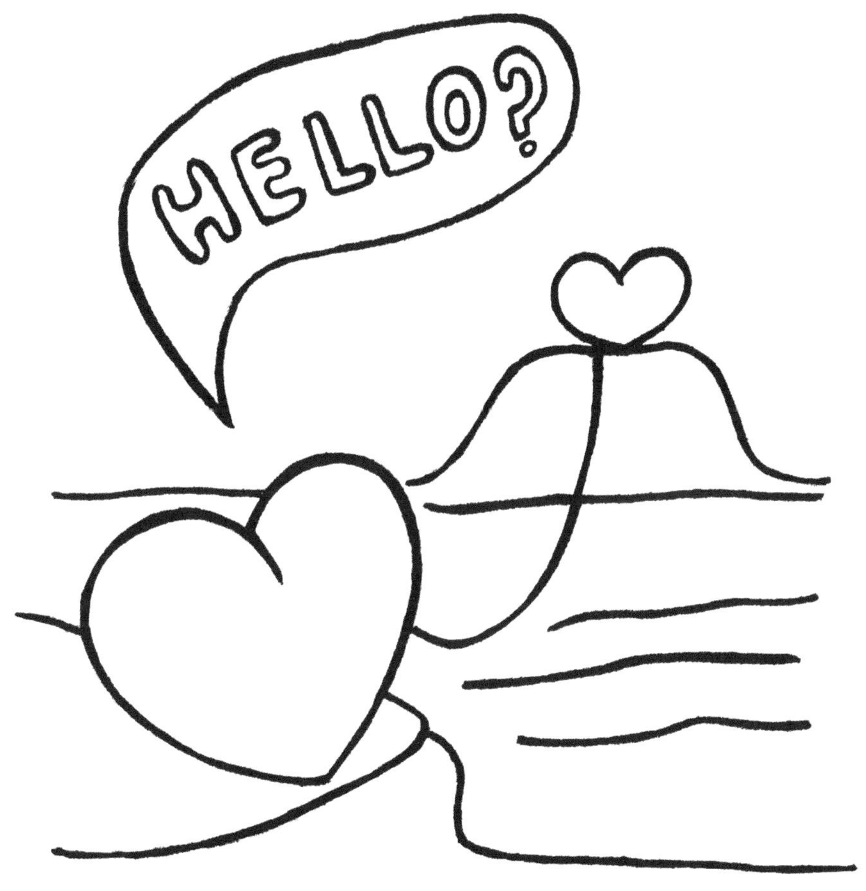

Far Away Love

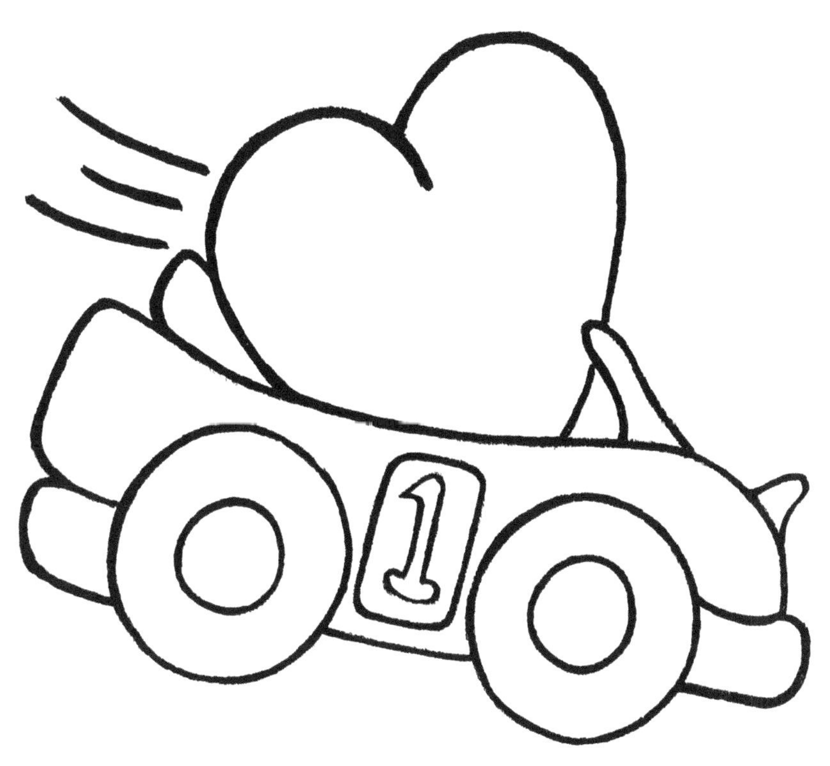

Ready, Set, Love!

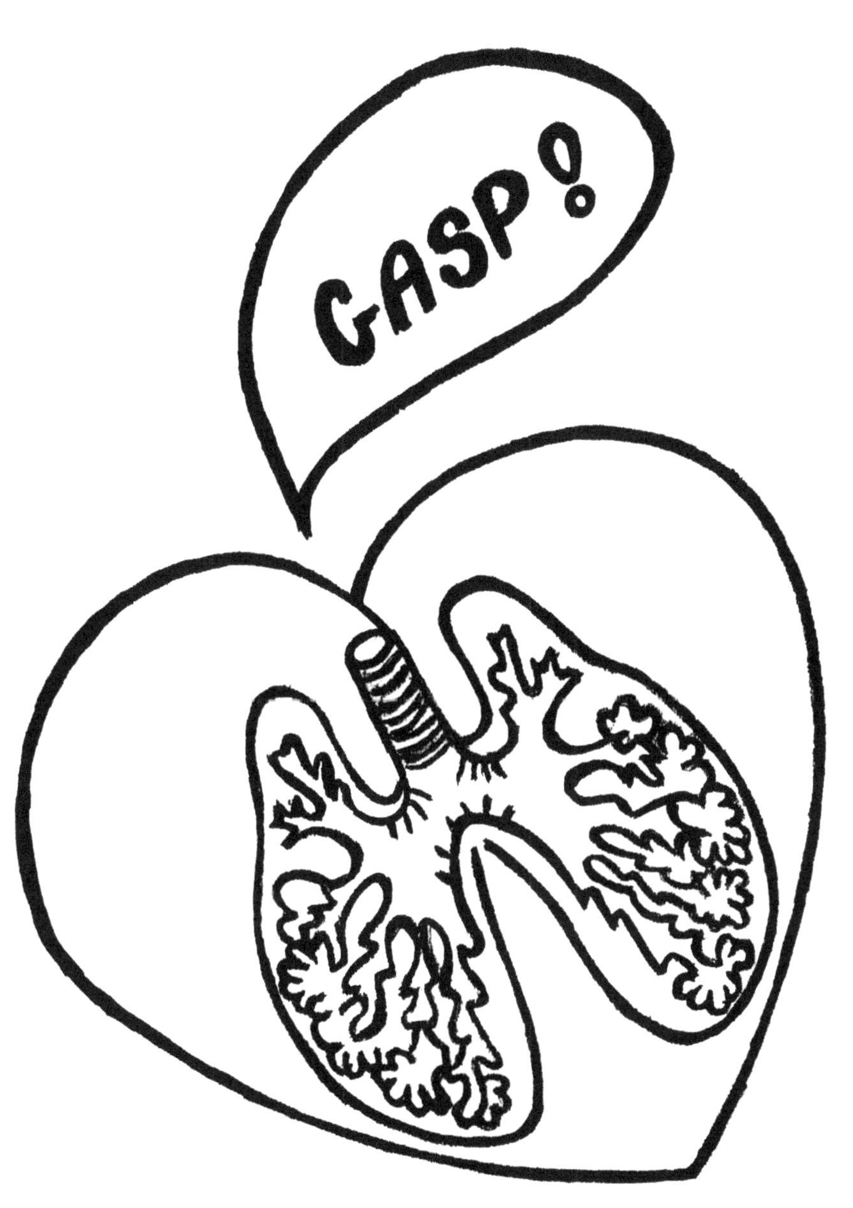

Breathless Love

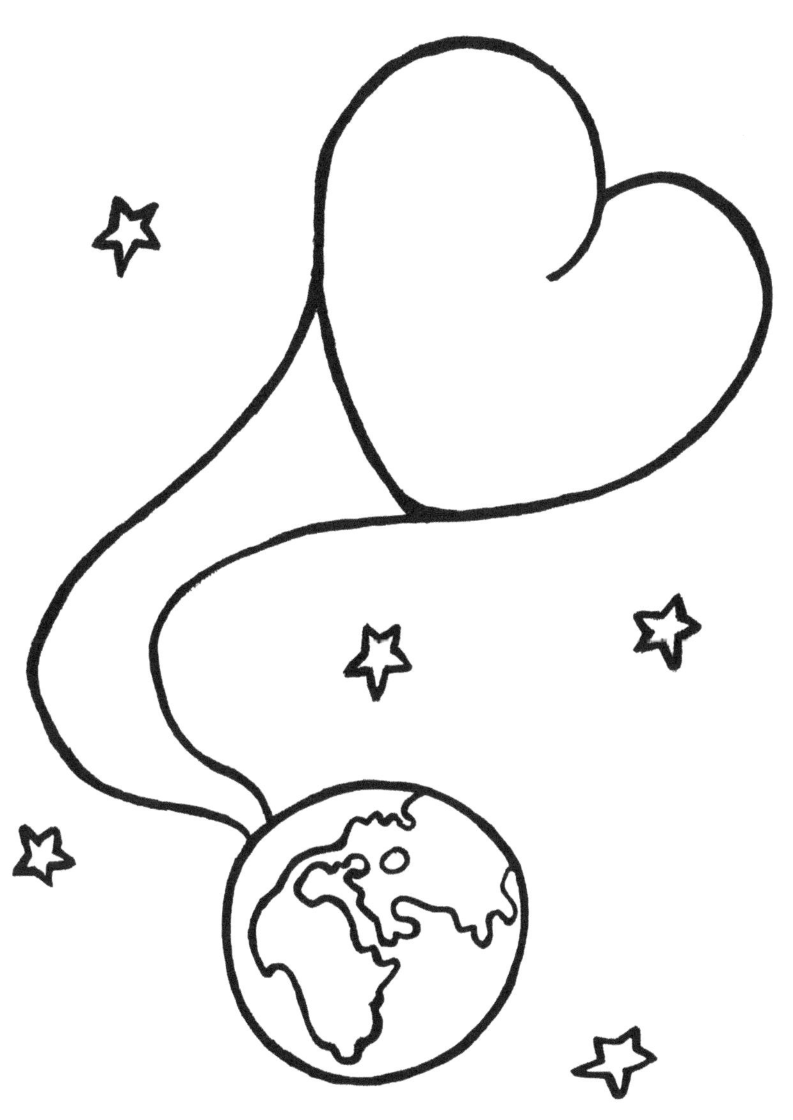

Out of this World Love

Love Blooms

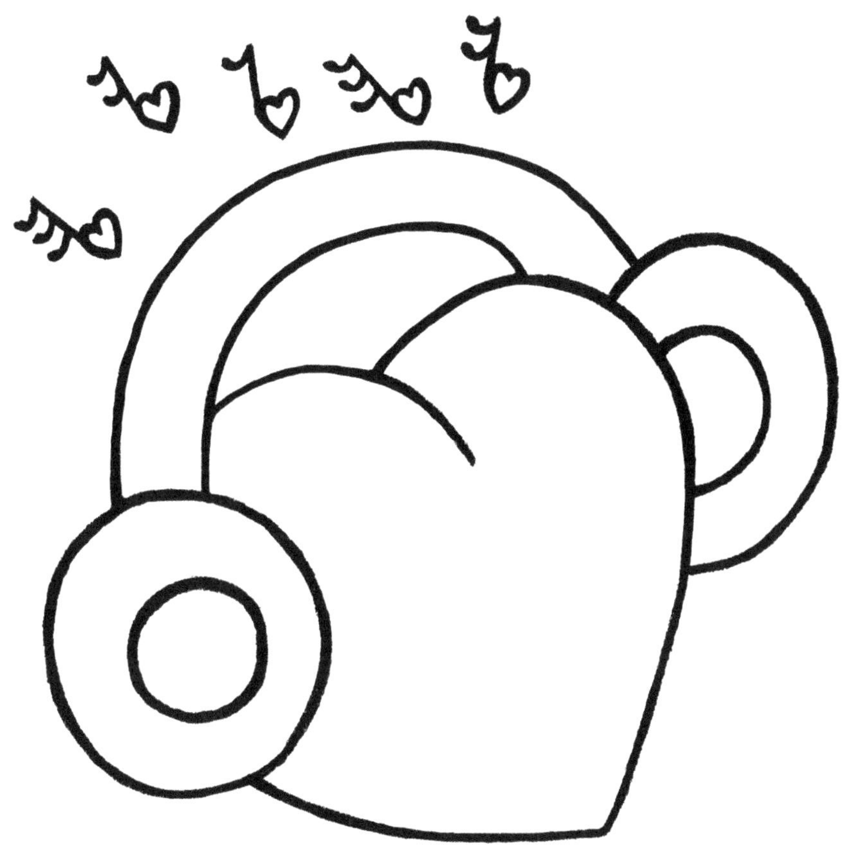

Listen to Love

Love Bandit

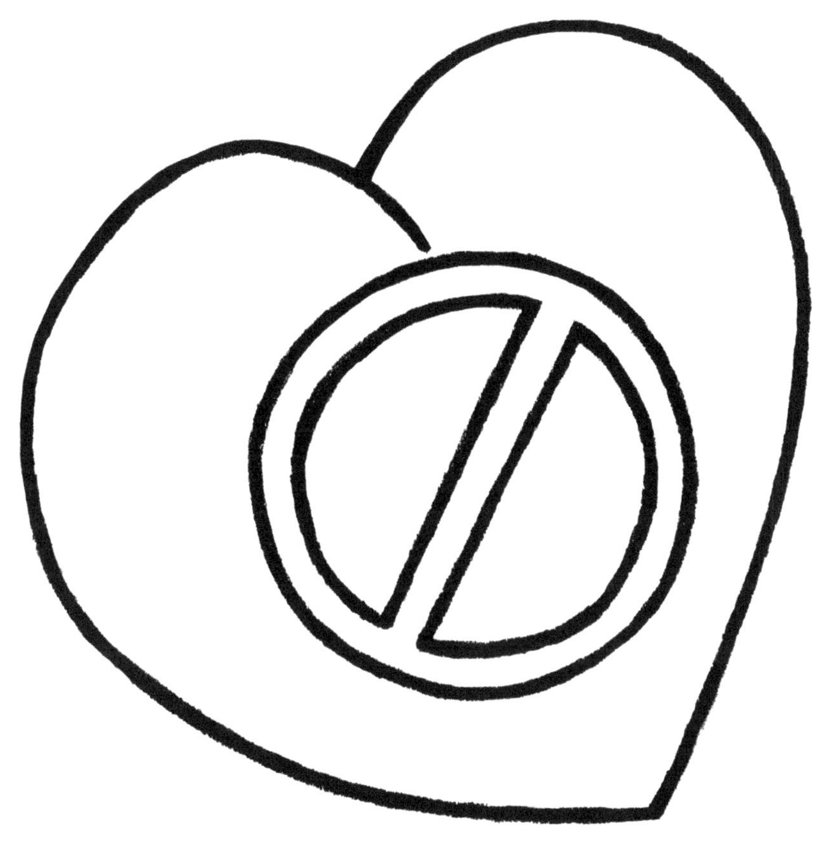

No Love

Honey Love

www.ingramcontent.com/pod-product-compliance
Ingram Content Group UK Ltd.
Pitfield, Milton Keynes, MK11 3LW, UK
UKHW020140250726
13967UKWH00002B/765

9 781948 172479